Accession no.
36195937

The Scholarship of Teaching and Learning in Higher Education

SRHE and Open University Press Imprint

Helping Students to Learn Series

Series Editor: Rowena Murray

If academics are genuinely to develop as teachers throughout their careers, if they are to continue to produce innovations, they have to bring a scholarly orientation to teaching. This series will show them how to do that. It will teach them how to make credible cases for different forms of innovation, thus helping them to situate teaching centrally in their careers. It will also show them ways of solving students' problems and methods of helping their students to learn more effectively.

Rowena Murray: The Scholarship of Teaching and Learning in Higher Education

Forthcoming titles in 2009

Bill Johnston, *The First Year at University: Teaching Students in Transition*

Anne Lee, *Helping New Postgraduates: A Guide for Academics*

The Scholarship of Teaching and Learning in Higher Education

Edited by
Rowena Murray

LIS LIBRARY

Date	Fund
8-5-15	Iki-che

Order No

2596945

University of Chester

McGraw Hill

Society for Research into Higher Education
& Open University Press

Open University Press
McGraw-Hill Education
McGraw-Hill House
Shoppenhangers Road
Maidenhead
Berkshire
England
SL6 2QL

email: enquiries@openup.co.uk
world wide web: www.openup.co.uk

and Two Penn Plaza, New York, NY 10121—2289, USA

Copyright © Rowena Murray 2008

All rights reserved. Except for the quotation of short passages for the purpose of
criticism and review, no part of this publication may be reproduced, stored in a
retrieval system, or transmitted, in any form or by any means, electronic,
mechanical, photocopying, recording or otherwise, without the prior written
permission of the publisher or a licence from the Copyright Licensing Agency
Limited. Details of such licences (for reprographic reproduction) may be obtained
from the Copyright Licensing Agency Ltd of Saffron House, 6–10 Kirby Street,
London, EC1N 8TS.

A catalogue record of this book is available from the British Library

ISBN-13: 978-0-33-5234462 (pb) 978-0-33-5234455 (hb)
ISBN-10: 0-33-523446-1 (pb) 0-33-523445-3 (hb)

Typeset by Kerrypress, Luton, Bedfordshire
Printed and bound by CPI Group (UK) Ltd, Croydon, CR04YY

Fictitious names of companies, products, people, characters and/or data that may
be used herein (in case studies or in examples) are not intended to represent any
real individual, company, product or event.

The *McGraw-Hill* Companies

CONTENTS

Contributors

Rowena Murray, University of Strathclyde

Marian McCarthy, University College Cork

Ian Finlay, University of Strathclyde

Christine Sinclair, University of Strathclyde

Barry Stierer, University of Westminster

Helen Fallon, National University of Ireland, Maynooth

Jacqueline Potter, Trinity College, Dublin

Matthew Alexander, University of Strathclyde

Diana Kelly, Higher Education Consultant/Educational Developer, USA

Glynis Cousin, University of Wolverhampton

Sarah Skerratt, Scottish Agricultural College, Edinburgh

Ruth Lowry, University of Chichester

Introduction

Rowena Murray

Rationale

The number and type of courses on teaching and learning in higher education (HE) are growing. These courses are now compulsory elements in new academics' careers. This creates a need for good material to support the development of university teachers. There is now a need to define the nature of scholarship of teaching and learning (SoTL) and demonstrate the qualities of scholarship in ways that make it meaningful to academics across the disciplines.

Growth in research and scholarship in SoTL has increased the range and depth of material available. What is needed now is a distillation of this material to support new lecturers in developing their knowledge and practice. In addition, new lecturers now face the challenge of understanding SoTL as a discipline in its own right. In light of these developments, there is a widespread need for texts that bring together established research and the body of good practice, bridging the theory–practice divide.

While the idea of a 'scholarship' of teaching and learning in HE is relatively new, and while SoTL is less mature, in some respects, than scholarship in many other disciplines, authors in this series have been working in this area for a considerable time. They were selected for their accumulated knowledge not only of SoTL, but also of the types of support university teachers request and value. These authors have experience not only of innovating in teaching and learning themselves, but also of supporting others in innovating. All the authors have extensive experience in staff and educational development:

- They are experts in their areas
- They have a body of knowledge and material, developed over years, refined in workshops, accredited courses and/or publications
- They include practitioners' debates about innovation-in-practice
- They address audiences across discipline boundaries.

These authors – all of whom have published in higher education – are familiar with the process of seeing university teachers through the innovation process.

Introduction to the series

The series title is 'Helping Students to Learn'. It is intended to appeal to university teachers, and researchers who teach, in three ways:

- First, each book emphasizes 'helping students' with what are known to be recurring problems or challenges in HE at this time.
- Second, the title 'Helping Students ...' indicates a practical, problem-solving approach. Academics in research intensive universities still have to teach well, and this series could save them time and effort, as they engage with institutional, and moral, imperatives, such as reducing student drop-out rates.
- Third, topics in this series were shaped by the authors' knowledge of current agendas in higher education and the ways in which these can improve teaching and learning. We interrogate and refresh concepts that professional and political groups bring to the discussion of HE teaching and learning.

This series will be of interest and practical use not only to those at the start of their careers but also to those who have a body of experience and knowledge, including those who have attended courses on teaching and learning in HE and who are motivated to improve the student experience. Above all, it will provide solutions to recurring challenges in learning at university.

This is not to say that university teachers need a 'grand tour' of the discipline of higher education studies, but theoretical underpinning is generally appreciated by staff on accredited courses in HE teaching and learning; it gets their attention. While they like to critique what constitutes 'research' and what they see as 'jargon', they recognize that when they move into what is, for them, a new field, they need to learn a new vocabulary and a new set of concepts. However, it is important to provide this intellectual apparatus in a concise and accessible form.

An additional challenge for university teachers, including those who have completed formal courses is to develop indicators of their continuing professional development (CPD). Most lecturers will agree in principle that their development as teachers does not end when they complete a course. Yet many are less sure about how to manage ongoing CPD in the teaching role: what comes after the initial HE teaching qualification?

If academics are genuinely to develop as teachers throughout their careers, if they are to continue to innovate, they have to bring a scholarly orientation to teaching. This series shows how to do that. It teaches lecturers how to make credible cases for different forms of innovation, thus helping them to situate teaching centrally in their careers. It will also, potentially, provide more of the stimulation that university teachers experience when they study teaching and learning at this level. With this knowledge, academics need not be spectators in the HE debate, but can further the development of SoTL.

Perhaps more importantly, the series will demonstrate ways of solving students' problems and methods of helping students to learn effectively. This series shows how, while solving some of the most important problems in teaching and learning, academics can be systematic, informed and above all rigorous in their approaches. Even university teachers who have completed accredited courses find that their students still have problems. No course provides all the answers.

What this series does not do is treat each element of the curriculum separately – course design, assessment, evaluation of teaching, etc. That approach has been fully articulated by others. Neither is this series a kind of guide to 'doing teaching quality assurance', although it has relevance to that process. Instead, it addresses elements of the curriculum in an integrated way, thereby educating readers in approaches that might help with other problems that are not covered in this series.

The authors and editor have a genuine desire to help university teachers, including researchers who teach, improve the student experience by:

- Developing coherent approaches to recurring challenges that students face
- Sourcing practical solutions in research and scholarship
- Sustaining innovation and performing well consistently
- Evidencing the impact of innovations, thereby enhancing knowledge and practice.

This series may also have further impact on readers' ability to mentor teaching assistants, novice lecturers or teachers recruited or seconded from other professions.

Central themes

Each title in the series will have three themes:

- Bridging the theory–practice divide
- Providing scholarly approaches to teaching and learning that are accessible and focused
- benefiting from the knowledge, background and materials of experienced staff and educational developers.

What is new about this series is that it addresses a familiar subject in new ways:

- Shifting the focus to scholarly activities that university teachers can perform

- Combining focus on selected topics with generalizability to other topics
- Equipping university teachers genuinely to develop throughout their careers, using a range of different activities, perhaps at different points in their careers.

Introduction to this book

The first book in the series is *The Scholarship of Teaching and Learning in Higher Education*. It is a 'keystone' volume for the series in the sense that it gives the reader the information they need to become scholars of teaching and learning.

Aims of this book

- To explore the meaning and nature of the scholarship of teaching and learning in higher education from a range of perspectives
- To analyse the forms and characteristics of this scholarship in practice
- To introduce the theoretical underpinnings of a scholarly approach, directing readers to a range of perspectives in the literature
- To discuss the purpose and value of scholarship in this area
- To define and demonstrate scholarly approaches in this context
- To propose strategies for continuing professional development in this area
- To prompt readers to take a strategic approach to their development as teachers
- To encourage and enable contributions to the scholarship of higher education teaching and learning from across the disciplines.

Who are the scholars of teaching and learning?

SoTL is a complex and ill-defined movement which contains at the same time the notion of enhancement for the benefit of collective and individual practice, and the concerns for better rewards for 'individual teaching efforts' [Kreber, 2003: 95]. Regardless of its emphasis, SoTL – in its many shapes and interpretations – is a major tool in rebalancing the teaching and research nexus [D'Andrea and Gosling, 2005: 160]. (Fanghanel, 2007: 200)

Debating whether or not SoTL is a 'movement' may be less important for most academics than recognizing its role in providing a framework and a literature for their development as teachers. One effect of using the concept of 'scholarship' in relation to teaching is that, as in other disciplines, it makes clear where responsibility lies: SoTL is the work of every university teacher.

This is an exciting time for this rapidly developing area. Academics in a range of disciplines can play a role in that development. Moreover, contributing to the development of SoTL is an important way of maintaining and refreshing academics' knowledge. This book will help them to do that.

Summary of this book

The book begins with an overview of the SoTL literature, including key contributors to the field and the main debates. Other chapters introduce definitions, concepts, resources and guidance for the lecturer-as-student in this area. There is a chapter on interactions between readers' home disciplines and SoTL, including knowledge, conceptions and paradigms.

Mid-way through the book there is a chapter on the practitioner's perspective, outlining a new lecturer's engagement with SoTL. This is followed by a group of chapters on evaluating teaching and learning and evidencing scholarship, including research methods for small-scale studies in this area.

Finally, the processes of demonstrating and contributing to scholarship in this area are described, with guidance on writing for publication in SoTL and higher education journals.

1

The scholarship of teaching and learning in higher education: an overview

Marian McCarthy

Introduction

> In scholarship and research having a problem is at the heart of the investigative process; it is the compound of the generative questions around which all creative process and activity revolves. But in one's teaching a 'problem' is something you don't want to have, and if you have one, you probably want to fix it ... Changing the status of the problem in teaching from terminal remediation to ongoing investigation is precisely what the movement for the scholarship of teaching is all about. (Bass, 1998–99)

Bass hits at the heart of the 'tired, old teaching versus research debate' (Boyer, 1990: 16): as university teachers we have inherited a culture that defines our research and status in terms of our discipline and relegates our teaching to some neutral transmission zone, lived out in what Shulman (1993) calls 'pedagogical solitude'. In this model a 'problem' in one's teaching is defined as a deficit; there is something wrong that must be 'fixed'. This in turn draws on a technical model of teaching to 'fix' it, thereby perpetuating the model of 'terminal remediation'.

Brew (2007) provides interesting insights on the teaching–research relationship, which throw light on why teaching and research have been polarized in this way. The traditional relationship between teaching and research is that they have inhabited separate domains (Brew, 2006: 18). 'Research' has been seen as taking place in a disciplinary research culture in which 'academics, researchers and postgraduate research students carry out the job of generating knowledge', whereas 'teaching is viewed as taking place within a departmental learning milieu' (Brew, 2007: 1), where teachers transmit knowledge. A graphical representation of this model suggests that teaching and research are, in fact, 'pulling in opposite directions' (Brew, 2006: 18), and that their separate domains work in competition with each other for 'time, resources and space' (Brew, 2007: 1).

Many academics will be able to identify with the deficit thinking behind this model: time spent teaching is time taken from research. However, a different concept of teaching lies at the heart of the scholarship of teaching and learning (SoTL) 'movement' (Hutchings, 2004); it sees teaching as intellectual work, as a process of inquiry, as research that employs the same criteria as other forms of disciplinary research; as 'ongoing investigation' that is made visible, shared with others, peer reviewed and published (Shulman, 1999).

This chapter provides an overview of the literature on the SoTL, with particular reference to its emergence in the 1990s in the work of the Carnegie Foundation for the Advancement of Teaching in the United States. It explores different definitions of scholarship, looks at its theoretical underpinnings, summarizes some key developments and highlights some of the key debates.

The origins of SoTL

The story of how SoTL began is worth telling, not only because it gives teaching its rightful place in universities, colleges or institutes, but because it puts the focus on what good teaching is all about: student learning and the search for its compelling evidence. Though popularized in the publication of *Scholarship Reconsidered* in 1990, by Ernest Boyer, then president of the Carnegie Foundation for the Advancement of Teaching, the concept of a 'scholarship of teaching' existed long before Boyer coined the term. For example, in 1928, in his inaugural address as President of the University of Chicago, Hutchins suggested that all departments should carry out experiments in undergraduate teaching and learning – a fundamental activity of SoTL – and that PhD students should be involved in this process and not just let loose on the 'helpless undergraduates' (www.issotl.org/tutorial/sotltutorial/home.html). Hutchins' words are still visionary and pertinent. They speak to current efforts to develop graduate education to include teaching as an intrinsic part of research and research training.

Though Boyer's (1990) work on the scholarship of teaching has received most attention, McKinney (2004: 3) points out that others contributed to the earlier discussion of the concept. For example, Shulman (1987) coined the phrase 'pedagogical content knowledge'. Pellino, Blackburn and Boberg (1984) discussed multiple forms of scholarship, including the scholarship of pedagogy, while products, such as course content and activities, were seen as a form of scholarship in Braxton and Toombs' (1982) research. Indeed, it was Eugene Rice, as a scholar in residence at the Carnegie Foundation, who originally came up with the blueprint for the four scholarships (Edgerton, 2005: xii).

What is important, however, is that the idea of having to redefine and realign scholarship was inevitable. As Edgerton (2005: xiii) points out, had *Scholarship Reconsidered* never been published, 'faculty priorities would still have surfaced as a major issue. The conditions under which colleges and universities do business were clearly changing'. What is paramount in terms of the development of scholarship at that time was that *Scholarship Reconsidered* spoke to academics 'not in their roles as "professors" (members of a university), but as "scholars" (members of an intellectual community)' (Edgerton, 2005: xii). In terms of the future development of SoTL, this distinction is crucial in underscoring the idea of teaching as 'community property' (Shulman, 1999) and foregrounding the idea of a 'teaching commons' (Huber and Hutchings, 2005).

Boyer's paradigm of scholarship

In *Scholarship Reconsidered: Priorities of the Professoriate,* Boyer (1990) set out to reconsider the role of the faculty, so that all roles and responsibilities could be valued equally. His vast experience at all levels in the education system had taught him much about the nature of the teaching role, its relationship to student-centred learning and the challenges for teachers embedded in an active learning model:

> ... faculty, as scholars, are also learners ... While well prepared lectures surely have a place, teaching, at its best, means not only transmitting knowledge, but transforming and extending it as well. Through reading, through classroom discussion, and surely through comments and questions posed by students, professors themselves will be pushed in creative new directions. (Boyer, 1990: 24)

Calling for a radical reappraisal of scholarship, Boyer argued that universities needed new forms of scholarship that moved beyond those of the traditional model of research. Boyer suggested four new, overlapping forms of scholarship: discovery, application, integration and teaching (Boyer, 1990: 16). This reappraisal had the potential to transform understandings of academic work: '*Scholarship Reconsidered* transformed the discussion. Instead of describing faculty roles in terms of the familiar trilogy of teaching, research and service, it argued that faculty were responsible for four basic tasks: discovering, integrating, applying and representing the knowledge of their scholarly fields' (Edgerton, 2005: xii).

Rice claimed that the primary intent was heuristic: 'to reframe the discussion about what faculty do as scholars on a broad range of fronts and to open up a lively conversation across higher education on this important topic' (O Meara and Rice, 2005: 17). In redefining the concept of scholarship, and questioning the dichotomy between teaching and research, Boyer

(1990: 15) began to bridge the teaching–research gap. He pointed out, for example, that the word 'research' was a recent addition to the language of higher education, used in England in the 1870s for the first time, to mark Oxford and Cambridge out as places of learning (research), as well as teaching. The term 'research' did not emerge until 1906, in American education.

Boyer (1990: 15) pointed to the richness of the term 'scholarship', which originally referred to a range of creative work, whose 'integrity was measured by the ability to think, communicate and learn', not by the number of publications a scholar produced, as has become the norm:

> Scholars are academics who conduct research, publish, and then perhaps convey their knowledge to students or apply what they have learned. The latter functions grow out of scholarship, they are not to be considered part of it. But knowledge is not necessarily developed in such a linear manner. The arrow of causality, can, and frequently does, point in both directions. Theory surely leads to practice. But practice also leads to theory. And teaching, at its best, shapes both research and practice. (Boyer, 1990: 15–16)

Boyer's argument (1990: 24) was that the teaching–research link needed to be reforged, and that a more inclusive view of what it meant to be a scholar was needed: 'a recognition that knowledge is acquired through research, through synthesis, through practice and through teaching' (Boyer, 1990: 24). In this new order there would be no hegemony; research, in the traditional sense, would be just one of four ways in which a scholar functions. If Boyer's message is to be taken seriously, it is now necessary to look closely at each of the scholarships and tease out their implications.

The scholarship of discovery

Investigative scholarship comes closest to what is traditionally understood by research, with its focus on publication. However, Boyer produced a new definition:

> The scholarship of discovery at its best contributes not only to the stock of human knowledge but also to the intellectual climate of a college or university. Not just the outcomes, but the process, and especially the passion, give meaning to the effort. (Boyer, 1990: 17)

In the new order, such scholarship also includes the creative work of scholars in the literary, visual and performing arts, hence the inclusion of all disciplines. Boyer's focus on the words 'process' and 'passion' highlight the creative and compelling nature of research. The question behind this kind of research is, 'What do I know and how do I know it?' This encompasses all aspects of research and investigation in all disciplines.

The scholarship of integration

Though he achieved his own doctoral degree in the traditional manner and was committed to traditional research, Boyer subsequently realized that scholarship required not just specialization, but integration. In proposing the scholarship of integration, Boyer highlighted the need for scholars to give meaning to isolated facts, analyses and observations, putting them in perspective and making connections within and between disciplines. This form of scholarship has much to do with purpose and goals of a general education.

As an academic dean, he began to question the overall purpose of the undergraduate experience and asked the question, 'And just what do we expect students to know and be able to do when they are handed a diploma?' (Boyer, 1990: 2). Indeed, such questions foreground the current focus across European universities on learning outcomes and the Bologna Agreement.

This scholarship suggests that the researcher as teacher needs to ask the question, 'How can the findings be interpreted in ways that provide a larger, more comprehensive understanding?' Boyer pointed out that the scholarship of integration is closely related to that of discovery. It involves, first, 'doing research at the boundaries where fields converge' (1990: 19). Such work, he suggested (1990: 21), is increasingly important as traditional disciplinary categories prove confining, forcing new categories of knowledge. The scholarship of integration, therefore, also includes the skill of interpretation, fitting one's own research – or the research of others – into larger intellectual patterns.

The scholarship of application

The third element, the application of knowledge, moves, in Boyer's terms (1990: 21) 'towards engagement', and, in the current literature, is referred to as the scholarship of engagement (Huber and Hutchings, 2005). Here, the scholar asks the questions, 'How can knowledge be responsibly applied to consequential problems? How can it be helpful to individuals as well as institutions? And, further, can social problems themselves define an agenda for scholarly investigation?' This is where theory meets practice and one informs and reforms the other.

Boyer provided interesting perspectives on the idea of service, central to this form of scholarship. He suggested that, too often, 'Service means not doing scholarship but doing good' (1990: 22). In order to be considered as scholarship, however, it would have to do more than that:

> Such service is serious, demanding work, requiring the rigor – and the accountability – traditionally associated with research activities ... The scholarship of application, as we define it here, is not a one way street ... New intellectual understandings can arise out of the very act of application ... In activities such as these, theory and practice vitally interact, and one renews the other. (Boyer, 1990: 22–3)

In short, the scholarship of application seeks ways in which knowledge can solve problems and serve the community. It implies the rigorous application of the scholar's expertise to 'consequential problems', which, in turn inform the discipline.

The scholarship of teaching

In relation to the scholarship of teaching, Boyer (1990: 23) cautioned that the 'work of the professor becomes consequential only as it is understood by others'. He therefore underlined the point that teaching is about learning. Teaching, in his terms, is not some 'routine function, tacked on, something almost anyone can do. When defined as scholarship, teaching both educates and entices future scholars' (Boyer, 1990: 23).

Boyer recognized that his committment to active learning and lifelong learning had implications for pedagogy:

> Teaching is also a dynamic endeavour involving all the analogies, metaphors, and images that build bridges between the teacher's understanding and the student's learning. Pedagogical procedures must be carefully planned, continuously examined, and relate directly to the subject taught ... knowing and learning are communal acts. With this vision, great teachers create a common ground of intellectual commitment. They stimulate active, not passive, learning and encourage students to be critical, creative thinkers, with the capacity to go on learning after their college days are over. (Boyer, 1990: 23–4)

Boyer articulated the intellectual work of teaching, an argument taken up by Shulman (1998): 'teaching, like other forms of scholarship, is an extended process that unfolds over time. It embodies at least five elements: vision, design, interactions, outcomes and analysis' (Shulman, 1998: 5).

'The new scholarship requires a new epistemology'

Kreber (2006: 114) suggests that SoTL was ready 'to come of age' in 1995 and points to the significance of articles in *Change* magazine in its development.

She highlights the work of Barr and Tagg (1995), who argued 'for a new paradigm for undergraduate education, one where the focus would be not so much on teaching but on learning' (2006: 114). She points also to the work of Donald Schön in interpreting the implications of Boyer's new scholarship: it demanded a new institutional epistemology, a new way of knowing and documenting evidence. Schön (1995) argued that methods of 'technical rationality', with their positivistic focus, were limited in their capacity to deal with the real problems of teaching and learning in 'the swampy lowlands'. He concluded that we needed 'a kind of action research', a reflective practice approach, in order to explore and understand student learning and professional practice.

Schön's thinking foregrounds the new methodologies and genres that were invented to harness problems that were 'messy, confusing and incapable of technical resolution' (Schön, 1995). By mapping out new territory, he paved the way for the use of teaching and course portfolios and evidence-based learning in the work of Bernstein (Bernstein et al., 2006), Cerbin (2000) and others. The work of Cross and Steadman (1996) was also influential at this time in building a solid foundation for the work of SoTL.

The contribution of *Scholarship Assessed*

Though Boyer's work was widely read and led to the intended, vibrant discussion needed around the concept of research as a multi-faceted scholarship, it left many questions unanswered. These concerned ambiguity surrounding the meaning of a scholarship of teaching in particular: was there a distinction between excellent teaching, scholarly teaching and scholarship of teaching? Another question emerged about how the scholarship of teaching aligned itself with the other scholarships. There was also the question of how these new forms of scholarship could and should be assessed.

It was in answer to the last question that *Scholarship Assessed: Evaluation of the Professoriate* was written in 1997. Here Glassick, Huber and Maeroff (1997: 25) argued that if all four scholarships were to be recognized and valued equally, then the same set of standards should apply to all of them. They identified the standards as follows: all scholarly work must have 'clear goals, require adequate preparation, make use of appropriate methods, produce significant results, demonstrate effective presentation and involve reflective critique'. These standards applied as much to the scholarship of teaching as to that of discovery; all must meet the criteria in order to be considered as scholarship.

Developing a scholarship of teaching and learning

Shortly after the publication of *Scholarship Assessed*, Lee Shulman, who replaced Boyer as President of the Carnegie Foundation for the Advancement of Learning, wrote an article entitled 'Taking Learning Seriously' (Shulman, 1999). Here Shulman developed the concept of a scholarship of teaching by further clarifying how it might be done:

> An act of intelligence or artistic creation becomes scholarship when it possesses at least three attributes: it becomes public, it becomes an object of critical review and evaluation for members of one's community; and members of one's community begin to use, build and develop those acts of mind and creation.

Shulman's definition emphasizes the idea that such scholarship would be accomplished only in the context of a community of scholars. This is the antithesis of 'pedagogical solitude' and the antidote to teaching as 'dry ice' (Shulman, 1993), i.e. as that which disappears without a trace, if not documented.

Shulman and Hutchings (1999) further developed the concept of SoTL in 'The Scholarship of Teaching: New Elaborations, New Developments', shifting the emphasis from teaching to learning:

> A scholarship of teaching is not synonymous with excellent teaching. It requires a kind of 'going meta', in which faculty frame and systematically investigate questions related to student learning – the conditions under which it occurs, what it looks like, how to deepen it and so forth – and do so with an eye not only to improving their own classroom but to advancing practice beyond it.

Thus, SoTL is not done only to publish and critique teaching, but, more importantly, to inquire into student learning. To the three criteria already named as characteristic of a scholarship of teaching (making teaching public, open to critique and evaluation and in a form others can build on) Shulman and Hutchings added a fourth, embedded in the other three: 'it involves question asking, inquiry and investigation, particularly around issues of student learning'.

From excellent teaching to scholarship of teaching

In the same article, it is clear that Hutchings and Shulman begin to draw distinctions between 'excellent', 'scholarly' and 'scholarship of teaching', aspects of the concept of SoTL that were missing from Boyer's definitions. Shulman and Hutchings (1999) lay out the parameters of the discussion as follows:

> ... *all* faculty have an obligation to teach well, to engage students and to foster important forms of student learning – not that this is easily done. Such teaching is a good fully sufficient unto itself. When it entails, as

well, certain practices of classroom assessment and evidence gathering, when it is informed not only by the latest ideas in the field but by current ideas about teaching the field, when it invites peer collaboration and review, *then* that teaching might rightly be called scholarly, or reflective, or informed. But in addition to all of this, yet *another* good is needed, one called a scholarship of teaching, which in another essay we have described as having three additional features of being public ('community property'), open to critique and evaluation and in the form others can build on.

Shulman and Hutchings (1999) do not presume that all faculty will wish to pursue such a scholarship, but they do see it as 'a mechanism through which the profession of teaching itself advances, through which teaching can be more than a seat of the pants operation'. However, they point out that the scholarship of teaching is a condition for excellent teaching and underline the long-term commitment necessary to bringing such scholarship about:

> It is important to stress that faculty in most fields are not, after all, in the habit of – nor do most have the training for – framing questions about their teaching and students' learning and designing the systematic inquiry that will open up those questions. Indeed one of the most fundamental hurdles to such work lies in the assumption that only bad teachers have questions or problems with their practice.

Conclusion

SoTL has its base in the disciplines, since all academics have a research discipline in which they are embedded. This is why SoTL is a 'big tent approach' (Huber and Hutchings, 2005) and reaches beyond the boundaries of educational research. Huber (2006: 72) points out that the disciplines have much to contribute to SoTL. She also indicates (Huber and Hutchings, 2005: 4) that 'there are elements of discovery, integration, and application within the scholarship of teaching and learning, because this work typically involves classroom inquiry, synthesizing ideas from different fields, and the improvement of practice, all at the same time'. Hence, the scholarships and disciplines are interdependent.

Hutchings (2004: 1) summarizes the progress that SoTL has made since 1990 by providing the evidence that now enables us to call it a 'movement', the core habits and commitments of which can be summed up as follows:

> that teaching is intellectual work, that student learning poses challenging problems that require careful investigation, that rich evidence about learning needs to guide thoughtful improvement and that the

important work of learning and teaching should not be allowed to 'disappear like dry ice' (Shulman, 1993) but be made visible, sharable and useful to others.

2

What's learning for? Interrogating the scholarship of teaching and learning

Ian Finlay

> ... the practices of learning in higher education cannot be separated from considerations of their purposes. Current ways of thinking about learning in higher education often appear to address questions of how people learn as if learning were a technique, method or even skill which can be applied to different situations irrespective of its wider purposes and context. (Rowland, 2006: 28)

This aim of this chapter is to explore the 'wider purposes and context' of learning in higher education. More specifically, the following questions will be addressed:

- What are universities for? Why do they exist? What are their purposes?
- What's learning for in higher education? What kinds of learning are appropriate in universities? What are different views of learning in higher education?
- What are possible outcomes of learning in higher education? How has one group of students described what they got out of a university course?
- What implications do the reflections offered on the above questions have for teaching and teachers in higher education?

The stance taken in this chapter is that learning and teaching in universities are social and moral practices, not just techniques, methods or skills that can be developed without consideration or understanding of the cultures of which they are part. The use of the plural 'cultures' is deliberate. There are many cultures in modern higher education, and new university teachers become inducted into a culture that is locally, institutionally and disciplinarily specific, in spite of apparently sharing features with other localities, institutions and disciplines.

If this is the case then how can a chapter such as this have anything to say about the generality of higher education? Indeed, is there a generality? The argument proposed here is that there is no generality to describe, but framework questions and reflections can be presented to assist new higher education teachers to explore their views and to draw their own conclusions about the what's and why's of teaching and learning as well as the how's that are explored elsewhere in this book.

This chapter engages with the scholarship of teaching and learning, by locating it in a wider scholarship that explores the nature and purposes of higher education.

What are universities for?

The discussion in this section centres on Newman's seminal text *The Idea of a University* (1976 [based on 9th edition of 1889]). In discourse VII Newman attacks the notion of education for work as being relevant to the mission of universities. The debate around the issue of whether universities exist to serve economic purposes, in the sense that they are to provide an appropriately trained professional workforce, or for cultural and personal enlightenment purposes is an old one. That this debate has contemporary relevance is illustrated by the way in which Newman's title has been adopted and adapted by recent writers, continuing to take up the issues he addressed (Daiches, 1964; Jaspers, 1965; Barnett, 1990; Pelikan, 1992; Maskell and Robinson, 2001).

Liberal versus professional education

In discourse VII, 'Knowledge Viewed in Relation to Professional Skill', Newman takes issue with ideas on education originally expressed by Locke (1693) in *Some Thoughts Concerning Education*. Locke promoted the concept of an education 'likeliest to produce, virtuous, useful, and able men in their distinct callings' (Locke, 1693, dedication) and further 'since it cannot be hop'd he [the student] should have time and strength to learn all things, most pains should be taken about that which is most necessary and that principally look'd after which will be most and frequentest use to him in the world' (Locke, 1693: part VI, section 94).

Newman would probably have accepted the first of these quotations. Where he took real issue with Locke was in the latter's criticism of teaching Latin, particularly through the construction of Latin verses. This criticism, later taken up by Edgeworth (1809) and the *Edinburgh Review* in the mid-nineteenth century, annoyed Newman. For Newman classical languages and poetry were at the centre of a liberal education. He was not opposed to the concept of usefulness of a university education, but he saw utility as one outcome of a liberal education rather than as the sole aim of a professional education. In Newman's view the object of a liberal education is to train the mind. Individuals with trained minds could then take up any occupation available, since they would have the mental apparatus necessary to cope with it:

> ... general culture of the mind is the best aid to professional and scientific study, and educated men can do what illiterate cannot; and the man who has learned to think and to reason and to compare and to discriminate and to analyse, who has refined his taste, and formed his judgement, and sharpened his mental vision, will not indeed at once be a lawyer, or a pleader, or an orator, or a statesman, or a physician, or a good landlord, or a man of business, or a soldier, or an engineer, or a chemist, or a geologist, or an antiquarian, but he will be placed in that state of intellect in which he can take up any one of the sciences or callings I have referred to, or any other for which he has taste or special talent, with an ease, a grace, a versatility, and a success, to which another is a stranger. In this sense then ... mental culture is emphatically *useful*. (Newman, 1976: 145)

For Newman, a good education is always useful, but a useful education is not always good.

Even in Newman's time *literae humaniores* was not the only course of study at his alma mater, Oxford. In a significant passage Newman tried to integrate professional studies with his concept of a liberal education:

> If then I am arguing, and shall argue, against Professional or Scientific knowledge as the sufficient end of a University Education, let me not be supposed ... to be disrespectful towards particular studies, or arts, or vocations, and those who are engaged in them. In saying that Law or Medicine is not the end of a University course, I do not mean to imply that the University does not teach Law or Medicine. What indeed can it teach at all, if it does not teach something particular? It teaches *all* knowledge by teaching all *branches* of knowledge and in no other way. (Newman, 1976: 147)

The terms of Newman's argument are similar to current debates on key/core/transferable skills. These may be the modern equivalent of Newman's training of the intellect. The debate continues about whether these are best developed in the context of subjects and disciplines, or whether they require specific, separate development. Newman was content for professional subjects to be taught in universities, provided they took a wide view and were used as a medium for delivering the liberal education he sought.

Although he has been both heavily criticized by some writers and uncritically lauded by others, Newman is rarely ignored in such discussions. Modern commentators take a variety of views on the role of universities in professional education. For example, Maskell and Robinson (2001: 30) criticize Newman, not for his ideals on liberal education, but for muddying the waters by attempting to justify his programme of liberal education on the grounds of preparation for a profession. They consider that to be fudging the issue. Their preference is for a university education unsullied by vocational, professional or economic imperatives.

Ryan (1999) is another educational philosopher of the liberal school. Unlike Maskell and Robinson, he recognizes the legitimacy of university involvement in professional education:

> Almost all societies that have discussed the question [of liberal educa- tion] at all have contrasted liberal education with vocational education, and seen it as something to which ordinary people would not have access. Newman, interestingly and rightly, rejected the contrast. He thought one virtue of a liberal education was that its possessors could embark on an indefinite range of careers. But he saw that there was a distinction between liberal education and what we now term training. To wish everyone both to have the skills they require to earn a living, and to possess the sense of cultural ownership that was once the prerogative of the few, is a new, and maybe impossible ambition. (Ryan, 1999: 31)

Gray (1999: 5) follows the tradition of Locke and Edgeworth in proposing a utilitarian mission for universities. Indeed, he argues that the idealistic and normative perspective of the likes of Newman suggest a university that never existed. He writes that 'the majority of universities in the UK were in fact established to fulfill economic functions. That meant they were in- tended to further the local development of trade and industry and to enhance the capability of members of the professions (new and historic)'.

The quotations above mix the prescriptive and the descriptive; comments on what ought to be stand alongside comments on what is or has been. Whitehead (1950) pointed out that universities have always mixed 'pure abstract learning' with professional learning. He pointed out that 'the University of Salerno in Italy, the earliest of European universities, was devoted to medicine', a Cambridge college was founded in 1316 for the purpose of 'providing clerks for the King's service' and training for the ministry, for medicine and for engineering has traditionally been provided by universities (Whitehead, 1950: 137–8).

What kind of education?

It may be more relevant to discuss the kind of education provided by universities, rather than to engage in a debate about professional versus liberal education. In a sense this issue has been empirically settled. Univer- sities provide liberal, general education and professional education. There was no golden Hellenic age when liberal education alone was provided, although the range of professions provided for by universities has greatly expanded.

Both Whitehead (1950) and Ryan (1999) provide views of the kind of education universities should provide. Whitehead suggests that,

> The justification for a university is that it preserves the connection between knowledge and the zest for life, by uniting the young and the old in the imaginative consideration of learning. The university imparts information but it imparts it imaginatively. At least this is the function it should perform for society. (Whitehead, 1950: 139)

Ryan (1999: 167) writes that, 'One of the central purposes of education is to overcome the sense of being "thrown" into a meaningless world'. This is to implicitly accept the constructivist position that creating meaning in the world in which one finds oneself, helped in some cases by those in the formal education system, is a core human drive. Rowland (2006: 17) concedes that the two views of the purpose of the university exist, but that they 'exist in tension and are, in fact, both present at any time'. He proposes the idea of the 'enquiring university':

> ... [which] would speak of itself in terms that are more closely rooted in the human values that it seeks to promote. Such values reflect the needs of employment in an enlightened democratic society as well as the values of intellectual enquiry. We must therefore be wary of any simplistic dichotomy between intellectual and vocational purposes. (Rowland, 2006: 6)

Interrogating the purposes of academic work and the work of departments and institutions is something that both new and experienced higher education teachers turn to periodically. The issue is rarely resolved at one go, but is revisited, as new policies appear, for example. Individual lecturers' positions in this debate may be strongly held or may be provisional, developing with each interrogation.

What's learning for?

Linked to the discussion in the previous section, the core issue of this chapter is the purpose of learning in higher education. Different scholars have produced different answers to this question. For example, Bowden and Marton (1998) argue that 'learning is the defining element of the university', and they develop this point by discussing two main types of learning in universities: learning undertaken by students, which they call individual learning, and learning undertaken through research by university staff, which they call social learning (Bowden and Marton, 1998: 4–5).

Bowden and Marton adopt a fairly functionalist approach to the purpose of learning. They suggest that 'institutional forms of learning such as studying at university ... are supposed to prepare students for handling situations in the future' (Bowden and Marton, 1998: 6). They argue that this involves being led along paths already familiar to the teachers; in other words, although knowledge gained from learning experiences may be new to students, it is not new to their teachers. Ramsden (2003) suggests that:

> ... learning in educational institutions should be about changing the ways in which learners understand, or experience, or conceptualize the world around them. The 'world around them' includes the concepts and methods that are characteristic of the field of learning in which they are studying. (Ramsden, 2003: 6)

These definitions capture part of what learning in higher education is about: it is about getting a new perspective of the world and drawing on the knowledge and experience of university tutors. It is about a formal, upfront and predictable curriculum. It is about learning what is stipulated in course and module descriptors.

Other authors, however, argue that learning in higher education is about more than this: learning is not just about coming to know the world around one, but also coming to know the world within oneself. It is not just about getting to know the world, but also about getting to know how to change the world for the better. Thus, there should be deep emotional engagement with learning, not just deep cognitive engagement. Some of these aspects may not be captured in learning outcomes, but they do happen. For example, Walker (2006) reports that: 'Martha Nussbaum believes that the job of a university teacher ... is to make human life better. She writes that becoming an educated citizen in and through higher education ... means acquiring knowledge and analytical skills but also 'learning how to be a human capable of love and imagination' (Walker, 2006: 3).

Walker herself argues that the purpose of learning in higher education is to develop human capability to 'lead more worthwhile and free lives' (Walker, 2006: 20). This aim is reflected in the words of an English sixth-form student: 'By going to university I hope to gain knowledge that will help me to contribute to making the world a better place' (Rowland, 2006: 6).

Metaphors for learning

Anna Sfard (1998) used the concept of discourses to classify ideas about learning. She used the idea of theory as metaphor and suggested that there are two main metaphors for learning: the acquisition metaphor and the participation metaphor.

For the acquisition metaphor the goal of learning is individual enrichment. Learning is seen as the acquisition of something, and the student is a recipient or reconstructor of knowledge. The teacher is provider, facilitator or mediator. Knowledge is seen as a property or commodity that can be possessed. Knowing is having or possessing. Thus, there is an emphasis in this metaphor on what Eraut (1994) calls public propositional knowledge, what Polanyi (1958, 1959) refers to as explicit knowledge, and what Blackler (1995) calls encoded knowledge. The acquisition metaphor can be seen in many contemporary accounts of university learning. For example, the work of Marton and Säljö (1976), Entwistle (1988), Prosser and Trigwell (1999), Biggs (2003) and Ramsden (2003) rely on the assumptions of the acquisition metaphor. They attempt to explain the learning of subject matter or of concepts relating to particular disciplines.

For the participation metaphor the goal of learning is community building. Learning involves becoming a participant, and the student is conceived of as an apprentice or peripheral participant. The teacher is an expert participant and preserver of practice. Knowledge is an aspect of practice, activity or discourse, and knowing is belonging, participating or communicating. Thus, examples of the participation metaphor are Polanyi's tacit knowledge, Blackler's embedded and embodied knowledge and Eraut's private and procedural knowledge. Accounts of learning that embody the assumptions of the participation metaphor include Lave and Wenger's (1991) situated cognition and contemporary versions of activity theory (Engeström, 2001).

One of the attractions of Sfard's position is that she neither selects one metaphor as superior nor attempts a synthesis, but suggests that both metaphors offer insights into the learning process. By drawing on both metaphors learning can be seen as individual sense-making through participation in a social activity or practice. This means that learning has two main dimensions: on the one hand, learning can be seen as accessing the corpus of public, propositional knowledge and making it one's own through personal reconstruction, and, on the other hand, as coming to know a practice or activity through social engagement in that practice or activity. It is proposed here that education that embodies both of these dimensions is richer and fuller than one that involves only one of them.

In summary, it could be argued that learning in higher education has several purposes: to pass on the disciplinary knowledge from one generation of scholars to the next, to help students gain an understanding of the world around them and of the world within themselves and to help them gain an appreciation of how they can improve the world and themselves. These purposes are achieved through both the acquisition of formal knowledge and skills and participation in a community of scholars.

What are possible outcomes of learning in higher education?

Several years ago I conducted a study of further education (FE) lecturers who had completed a university teacher education course, aiming to assess its impact on them (Finlay, 2003). I classified their responses into two categories that I called 'internalist' and 'externalist' representations of learning. One group of participants reported that their experience of the course had changed them as people. This change was largely internal and transformative. The second group represented their experience quite differently. They saw themselves as having learned a set of skills, techniques or strategies that they then used with their students. They represented their practice as something external to themselves.

Internalist accounts of learning on the course displayed the following features:

- Constructivist approach to learning
- Concern with affective as well as cognitive development
- Viewing theory as something that developed their perspectives or changed their views of the world
- Valuing confirmation as person/practitioner of worth
- Viewing their profession as something they were rather than something they did
- Seeing tensions and paradoxes as part of learning.

Externalist accounts of learning on the course had the following features:

- Behaviourist approach to learning and practice
- Viewing theory as something to be applied or tried out in practice
- Viewing their profession as something they did rather than something they were
- Lacking explicit or implicit reference to or awareness of tensions or paradoxes
- Getting ideas or techniques from the course to apply in their own practice.

These two representations are concerned with the outcomes of learning for a group of students on a higher education teaching course, but they also reflect, in broad terms, views on the purposes of learning, the focus of this chapter.

Implications for teachers in higher education

This chapter started with a quote from Rowland in which he problematized the notion that university teaching and learning were only about the application of a set of techniques, skills and strategies. That is not to say that developing notions about deep and surface learning and about the different conceptions that learners have of learning and teachers have of teaching are not important to new teachers in higher education. The argument developed in this chapter is that things are a lot more complicated than that. Teachers not only help students to change and expand what they know; they are also involved in changing who they are. In a sense, just as teachers do not just teach what they know, they also teach who they are; so students do not just learn what they come to know, they also learn who they are.

This is why it was suggested above that teaching is a social and moral activity within a cultural context. The extent to which the issues raised in the previous paragraph impact on teachers will depend very much on the kind of teacher they want to be, whether they adopt internalist or externalist perspectives, whether they can combine different perspectives or theories in their teaching and on the institutional, disciplinary and departmental cultures in which they teach. Continuous engagement with the scholarships of teaching, learning and university purposes, as well as with disciplinary scholarship, continually refresh the idea of what it means to be a university teacher.

3

Lecturers as students – in a 'meaningful sense'

Christine Sinclair

Can staff/researchers ever really become students in any meaningful sense?

Some years ago, having completed a BA in philosophy and an MA in education, I decided to embark on a completely different course of study – a Higher National Certificate (HNC) in Mechanical Engineering in order to gain insight into the student experience. Having successfully completed the HNC, I was admitted to a level two module in Engineering Design as a 'direct entry' student. While I was a student, I was also researching students' responses to discourse practices, a study for which I subsequently achieved the award of PhD (Sinclair, 2004). Currently, this experience and research support my work with students and academic staff in the Centre for Academic Practice and Learning Enhancement (Sinclair, 2008).

I wrote a paper that used my own experiences of being a student on these courses, aiming to make some observations about practices in higher education. The reviewer's response quoted above suggests that some academics would not accept my experiences as authentic, despite my achievement of a qualification in Engineering. This raises interesting questions about the role and identity of a student, and about who 'counts' as a student. In particular, this reviewer seems to suggest that academics pass through some irreversible threshold to reach their current status and can never be students again.

What does this say about academics enrolling in their own university's postgraduate course in higher education studies or teaching? What is their position? They are usually not referred to as 'students', but as course participants, for example. Perhaps this usage is intended to distinguish lecturers from their own students – either to avoid confusion or to preserve their status. Yet many requirements of a course participant are identical to those of a student on a similar level of course. If you are taking such a course, you might want to consider what you would prefer to be called and what that means for your position.

This chapter suggests that – in addition to the value of any content – professional courses in higher education studies can offer insights about participation in university courses in general. However, it also takes account of an opposing view: that staff and students are so different in status, power and identity that conclusions about such an association may indeed not be 'meaningful' to all.

A rationale for connecting lecturers' and students' experience

The reason I had become a student again was because I was dissatisfied with some of the accounts of student experience in the literature in the academic discipline referred to here as 'higher education studies'. I wanted to discover whether direct observation of student experience would provide additional understanding of what happens in the classroom, and I was particularly interested – and still am – in what students actually do in terms of engaging with various discourses. My study produced uncomfortable but unsurprising findings: for example, students are not always doing what the courses and certification claim that they are doing. Nevertheless, there was evidence of what Barnett (2007) has called 'a will to learn' – most students persevere with and complete their studies. By being one of these students, I was in a position to view, from the inside, the environments, activities and relationships that can support this will to learn. I could take this knowledge forward to my own work with students and other course participants, including participants in courses on teaching and learning in higher education, which I have taught for many years.

The classroom for the subject 'higher education studies' will probably contain participants who hold a wide range of perspectives on the value of such courses and their own activities within them. If you are an academic taking one of these professional courses, you may find yourself in a room full of competing views on what should be happening. Indeed, given the critical stance expected in academic life (Barnett, 1997) it might be disappointing if that were not the case. The same, of course, is true of classrooms where you teach, and though young undergraduates will not necessarily express their views to you on what 'ought' to be going on, they will undoubtedly be expressing them somewhere. The different views of different participants are likely to contribute to each individual's understanding of the situation.

It is likely that lecturers taking a course in higher education studies will be expected *inter alia* to do the following: listen to someone talking about the topic, read texts, join in discussions, reflect on what happens in practice and write about some findings during the course. All of these activities are likely to happen at set times and according to some regulatory framework, resulting in some kind of warranty – for example, a certificate that permits progression through probation.

However, although it is easy to highlight that the activities and context are very similar, the analogy between lecturers and students may break down at the significant level of what has been termed 'the pedagogical relationship' (Bernstein, 1996; Barnett, 2007). A lecturer has achieved a certain status through rites of passage, including moving on from the student identity, and may not want to return to being a novice. The relationship between the lecturer and the educational developer who teaches a higher education module may be far removed from that between the lecturer and an undergraduate student. The following quotation from a lecturer studying on an educational development course encapsulates this difference: 'We've all taught before, of course. Most of us have been doing this work as part of making ends meet for some considerable time. And then you come along to tell us, with apparently no sense of irony, how to "get started". And who are you anyway?' (Ashforth et al., cited in Land, 2004: 131). The quotation goes on to include an acknowledgement from the participant that some lecturers – colleagues – may need this kind of work, but the language associated with the discipline of higher education teaching, especially its acronyms and abbreviations, has a tendency to make 'our eyes glaze over'. Questions to do with relevance, legitimacy of particular courses and the language used can arise for all students – I certainly heard my fellow students asking them in my engineering course. The 'Who are you anyway?' question addressed to educational developers may well resonate with other academics, for example those experiencing the 'impostor syndrome' (Brems et al., 1994).

What follows in this chapter aims to take account of lecturers' existing status and identity rather than to destabilize them. It is important, though, to acknowledge that some people in the higher education studies classroom may feel that their status or identity is being challenged, and may indeed have good reason to feel this, as will be suggested later. Awareness of such perspectives offers one explanation for some of the reactions that can occur in this classroom. Moreover, relationships with those who teach and assess courses, and concerns about identity are relevant for any classroom.

Case study: what a student notices about learning and teaching

The rationale above takes pains to stress that people in any higher education classroom (students or lecturers) are unlikely to form a homogenous group. They will have different expectations, views on their own status, habits from their previous academic practices and experiences, different responses to new language and terminology – and many other differences. It may, therefore, seem questionable to draw on a single student's experience to make the case for the value of putting oneself in a student's position. The aim, however, is not so much to promote the findings of my student experience; rather, it is to explore ways in which these findings helped me understand other classroom situations and shaped my responses to them.

Sometimes my experience appears anecdotal – perhaps offering reassurance to students who are struggling, or suggesting tactics that worked for me at the time. Sometimes, though, I have evidence for claims about classroom practice – claims that are rarely surprising but frequently forgotten by those who have become full members of an academic 'tribe' (Becher and Trowler, 2001). As a result of my research, I am able to show, for example, the relationship between a student's actions and his or her response to a particular classroom event, or to a troublesome concept, or to negotiating assessment requirements. I can demonstrate that things are not always as they seem in a classroom, or what they are warranted to be. I can also provide examples of barriers to progress and evidence of what is happening when the student perceives that he or she *is* progressing.

In my study I found these things out without any deception; I was not an 'undercover' student (unlike, for example, Nathan, 2005). However, if I had been intending to continue with my study of mechanical engineering, I might not now 'confess' so readily to some of my misunderstandings and ways of getting by. These observations would necessarily remain tacit and unavailable.

Of all the areas of my experience that provided useful information for my own practice, I have selected three that seem particularly pertinent to lecturers undertaking a professional course in higher education teaching. The first relates to institutional requirements for a course and how they balance with the rest of an academic's life; the second is to do with the academic discipline and especially its language; the third is about the difficulties of 'getting' key concepts in a new subject. Drawing on the results of my study I am able to make comparable observations about experiences of lecturers on professional courses in several institutions where I have been a course designer, facilitator, evaluator or external examiner.

Managing course workload in relation to other demands

I noted in my journal as a student that I had various excuses for being poorly prepared for a class test and assignment – I had a job interview, a meeting that required an overnight stay and had moved house, all in the same week. One of my colleagues said to me, 'I've every sympathy, but it won't wash, you know. You're a student, and if you came up with these reasons to me, I wouldn't accept it. You were told the dates of the test and the assignment'. I had to agree, but it was interesting to see from the other side what the genuine pressures on time meant for completion.

Because these were assessments, and there were penalties associated with not doing the work, I did use the little time I had available as well as possible. I can therefore see a value in the penalties, though I became aware that, for myself and my fellow students, compliance with assessment criteria made us very instrumental and possibly likely to emphasize regurgitation at the expense of deep thinking.

There is occasionally an irony in seminars on professional development courses when lecturers complain about their students not handing in work on time – and then suddenly realize that there is a parallel because they have not produced their own work for the current session. Sometimes, a wry smile or raised eyebrow from the facilitator is sufficient to make the point.

However, this is an opportunity to reflect on the relationship between deadlines and academic life. We can identify the 'costs' associated with missing a deadline: if it is one for a conference paper, for instance, then we might not be able to go to the conference. If it is for a chapter of a book, we might lose standing or credibility with editors/publishers.

For a professional course participant, failure to submit an assignment on time can have some of the same consequences as it would for any student – loss of face, failure to complete a course. The implications for a lecturer can be serious, especially if course completion is a probationary requirement. The point here is that there can be many potential consequences of non-compliance with course requirements – including some that will not matter very much in the circumstances and some that will be very serious indeed. That may depend on how tightly the regulatory framework is applied.

This observation has alerted me to the need for anyone taking a course to consider the implications of what they do and do not do, which may involve telling someone else about consequences of their inability to comply with university requirements. I have used this information to advise both students and lecturers.

If you are a student on a course in higher education studies, it might be useful to identify any barriers to meeting attendance requirements or submission dates. Highlighting the consequences of any difficulties in compliance puts you in a strong position to consider what actions need to be taken, which may of course involve discussions with other people, such as your head of department. It is also salutary to consider possible consequences of any lack of compliance for your own students: are these consequences 'real' and are they clearly stated? Can consistently applied consequences be used to achieve effects that you are seeking for your students?

Coping with alien terminology – and making the new 'meaningful'

As a mechanical engineering student, I struggled with some new words (such as 'enthalpy'), with abbreviations (the letter 'g' seemed to cause particular problems) and with the new significance of words and abbreviations that I already used (for example, I had to be very careful in my use of the words 'heat' or 'work'). In some subjects, the terminology can be associated with complex processes, pictures or numbers. I chatted to one of my lecturers who told me: 'I take it for granted that people know these formulae. They're just kicking about my head – work, torque etc.'.

I realized that I had my own equivalent expressions kicking about my head – educational jargon that might not mean very much to academics from some other disciplines. On one professional course, for example, when we asked some cross-disciplinary participants to identify 'critical incidents', lecturers expressed alarm at their different understandings of the expression, with some making associations with negative life experiences and others with nuclear reactions.

This alerted me to the need to draw attention to specialized language, including the consequences of using it. Students often worry about writing in the 'academic way', and I frequently see postgraduate students who move from one academic discipline to another and experience real difficulties in responding to the new language and, especially, in adopting it for their own use. Similarly, academic staff report problems in working on cross-disciplinary projects, when perhaps there is some jostling to determine which academic jargon will predominate. Whether it is new words or unfamiliar symbols in formulae, if the language does not fit with what you are used to, then there will be a challenge to your way of seeing the world.

The language and conventions of the subject will particularly come into focus when you have to write about it, as Barry Stierer exemplifies and problematizes in Chapter 4.

Key concepts – new subject

Being able to use a word like 'enthalpy' correctly entailed developing an understanding of complex properties and processes. I frequently struggled with this, even when I did already know the word. When I was an engineering student, I often spoke at lunchtimes with colleagues in engineering departments at my own institution. One had an exam question with him one day and asked me which direction I thought a force would be in. His colleague said: 'You can see her struggling with something that would come naturally to us'. The concept of force is, of course, vital to engineering, but is one that is known to cause problems (see, for example, Svensson,

1989). Students can pass appropriate assignments, but still revert to Aristotelian ideas about force when the context is changed. I have frustratingly little record of evidence of change in my ideas about force. I did, however, write a telling journal entry: 'my intention – even in my own personal diary – is not to articulate my understanding [of force] but to get it right'. In other words, I did not want to write anything that might be wrong, even if I was to be the only person who read it.

I use this insight in working with students who are reluctant to commit anything to paper and to talk to staff about the difficulties of eliciting anything from students that might be judged to be 'wrong'. But I have also encountered staff on professional courses with a similar reluctance to commit anything to paper. By reminding myself of my own concerns about producing something wrong, I am able to respond with sensitivity. This has alerted me to the risks involved when a person's sense of identity seems to be at stake.

There is a growing interest in and body of knowledge about 'threshold concepts' (Meyer and Land, 2003), concepts that provide transformations to people's ways of thinking and being. An understanding of force is one of these; a lecturer's understanding of professional practice in higher education teaching may be or may contain another. Threshold concepts are inherently troublesome and likely to involve a liminal state 'where previous learning is rendered less certain, more fluid, and open to transformation' (Land, 2004: 188). If the developer or teacher is acting in a way that opens up such a liminal space, the course participant or student is challenged in a way that may feel destabilizing. This goes beyond being sensitive to people who worry about being wrong and gets to the heart of making connections between teaching and learning.

If you are a participant on a professional course in higher education studies, you may want to try to avoid such liminal states by not engaging fully with the new language and concepts to which you are being exposed, but there are still risks that you will encounter the liminal spaces in your teaching.

Connecting teaching with learning

My intention here is not to dwell on barriers but to acknowledge them. As a student, I was ultimately successful: I achieved my HNC in mechanical engineering, and it provided a passport to a second level module in engineering, which I also passed. If you are a student on a professional course, you are likely to succeed eventually, especially if completing your probation depends on it. Most students do complete their studies, despite – or perhaps because of – the problems they face. It is then useful to emphasize what encourages students to persist and succeed.

As a mechanical engineering student, I had times of great difficulty and times when I felt I had made progress. Often these were connected, as I sometimes made progress by persisting through a difficult situation. I trawled my journal for examples of actions I was undertaking when I felt I was making progress. This produced a chronological list (Figure 3.1) that suggests there were hierarchical stages to be worked through in the duration of the course, even though the HNC course itself was modular. As well as a willingness to make errors, this list is underpinned by a strong sense of seeing myself developing within a community.

- Follow set procedures
- Imitate lecturer, text, fellow students
- Recognise errors
- Compare practices
- Recognise a specific procedure
- Identify principles of a subject
- Fill in gaps
- Discern variation in ideas and artifacts
- Give and receive peer support in a community
- Discuss abstract ideas
- Discuss engineering as a novice engineer
- Question and debate procedures
- Connect abstract and concrete ideas
- Conceptualise a situation on the basis of what is discovered in the discourse
- Revisit topics in a new context
- Identify an 'Engineering discourse' situation

Figure 3.1 A student's perceptions of actions at points of progress in a programme of study (Sinclair, 2004)

I have used the example in Figure 3.1 in other writing and also in introductory courses for new lecturers. It tends to elicit a strong response, along the lines of, 'It wouldn't occur to me that students had to go through the first four or five stages: my starting point is that they need to be able to identify the principles of a subject'. Some staff are concerned at the suggestion of imitation as an early sign of 'progress', which becomes the basis for a conversation about the stages at which students must move on from imitation. I find it helpful here to consider Vygotsky's distinction between imitation that is simply automatic copying and a more meaningful approach where imitation 'is the source of instruction's influence on development' (Vygotsky, [1934] 1987: 210–11). Students should not attempt to be mimics, but they do need role models. At the very least, they need a sense of what others do in similar circumstances. And, perhaps, academics do too.

Making meaning from the student experience

I am claiming, then, that acknowledging that an academic is sometimes in the position of a student will yield insights that can later be used in teaching. The value of this insight goes beyond empathizing with the logistical and temporal difficulties of doing a course, and even beyond the issues associated with coping with new knowledge from a new perspective. In educational jargon, the experience is not just epistemological, it is ontological as well. This means that a course does not just give students new knowledge; it also affects who they are. Ron Barnett summarizes this well when stressing the importance of standards in higher education: 'The student comes to an appreciation of the critical standards in question and so becomes self-critical; the critical voices are internalized, but in the process, those critical voices may bear in so penetratingly that they thwart just what is struggling to form itself, namely authentic being' (Barnett, 2007: 160). It is not difficult to substitute the word 'student' in the above statement with the words 'participant on a professional course'. In an environment beset with quality measures and targets, we can readily recognize these internalized critical voices. Barnett calls on us all to collaborate in self-critical communities, helping one another to emerge as authentic beings – both students and lecturers.

The decision to be a student of higher education teaching

Many staff do not make the decision to take a professional course in higher education studies; the decision is made for them. I have some sympathy with those who might resist or question this, even though I am promoting the value of the experience of being a student. If you are taking any higher education course, it would be better if you had a free choice to do so. You would probably say the same about your own students.

While you may not choose to take the course, you do have the freedom to decide whether you should regard yourself as a *student* on it or not. As a graduate, you have been through the thresholds of being a student in your discipline; as a postgraduate course participant, you may well face some further thresholds – and, arguably, if the course is any good, you probably should.

4

Learning to write about teaching: understanding the writing demands of lecturer development programmes in higher education

Barry Stierer

A stranger in a strange land

Lecturers in higher education (HE) taking part in a programme of teacher development, such as an accredited course on teaching and learning in higher education, are expected to write about teaching as part of their coursework. In this chapter I discuss some of the distinctive ways these programmes expect those who teach at university to write. It also provides guidance on how to interpret and meet those expectations, in the hope that this will make them less daunting, and so that participants can more easily enjoy the benefits of these programmes.

I have been closely involved in planning and running higher education lecturer development programmes for many years, and I have become increasingly aware of the difficulties many lecturers have in understanding and fulfilling the writing requirements of the courses, even when they are accomplished writers in their own disciplines. The courses require them to produce texts of considerable complexity, in which they switch from dispassionate conceptual analysis, to discussing links between theory and practice, to reporting the results of small-scale educational enquiry, to personal reflective analyses of their own development as teachers – often within the same piece of writing. Many courses require participants to use the very process of writing in new and unfamiliar ways – that is, as a tool for personal reflection rather than as a communication medium. Moreover, the guidance given for writing successfully is often expressed in language that can be baffling to many participants (e.g. 'You should write at Masters level').

Participants in these courses are often expected to write about their teaching using language and concepts from the field of higher education studies (HES). For many lecturers, this field can seem like a strange land – indeed as strange a land as a new subject area can be for typical university students (McCarthy, 1994). My aim in this chapter is to acknowledge this strangeness, and to help lecturers feel at home with the distinctive 'ways of knowing' that are used in this field of study.

In writing this chapter I have drawn on concepts and methods developed in an area of educational research known as 'academic literacies', which investigates aspects of students' reading and writing in higher education (see, for example, Lea and Stierer, 2000). My premise is that there is much to learn about the experience of higher education lecturers writing on lecturer development courses by applying some of the approaches and analyses that have emerged from studies of undergraduate and postgraduate student writing. I have also drawn on research into academic identities (see, for example, Henkel, 2000) and the research into cultures of disciplines in higher education (see, for example, Becher and Trowler, 2001).

'Ways of knowing' in higher education studies

I have used the metaphor of *a stranger in a strange land* to describe the experience of trying to understand and follow (and possibly challenge) the ground rules of HES. In some respects, and for many academics, this subject area might be even stranger than a new subject area can be for a university student. After all, few academic programmes admit students who have no prior experience of studying in the subject area – and possibly not much practical work experience in the field either.

Though it may seem obvious, the first essential step for anyone starting out on a lecturer development course is to acknowledge explicitly that they are crossing significant boundaries, and are beginning to study in a new and unfamiliar subject area. Just because it happens to be the discipline that has grown up around an important aspect of your professional role (teaching) does not mean that you will become adept at using the distinctive ways of knowing within HES without some effort. This is not to say that you need to become an 'educationist' in order to benefit from these ways of knowing. I believe that all lecturers in higher education should be encouraged to take a scholarly approach to their teaching – rather than view teaching as a set of technical skills that they can be trained to execute – a view that underpins all the chapters in this volume. However, this does not require you to become a specialist in the HES subject area.

Approaching HES as a new subject area means we can use what is known about the way academic disciplines operate to understand why HES appears the way it does from the outside. For example, one of the things that lecturers who are new to this field often say is that it is jargon-ridden and even pseudo-scientific. It is true that lecturer development programmes introduce lecturers to concepts, schools of thought and theoretical frameworks drawn from the field of education, which itself has drawn from such disciplines as psychology, sociology, history, philosophy, anthropology and management. Some of these concepts have nearly acquired the status of holy writ: 'deep and surface learning' (Marton and Säljö, 1997), 'constructive alignment' (Biggs and Tang, 2007), and 'reflective practice' (Schön, 1995) are prominent examples.

Educational terminology may strike you as gibberish, but I suspect many newcomers to your own discipline respond in similar ways. After all, one person's jargon is another person's precise and analytical terminology, developed over time to advance the field's ways of knowing. At the same time, however, specialized language also functions as a way of staking out territory for disciplinary tribes (Becher and Trowler, 2001), and of creating exclusive clubs that only admit fluent speakers. This applies to all disciplines, your own included, and HES is no exception.

HES is a practice-based and relatively new discipline, and there are 'tensions and conflicts over such issues as what counts as knowledge, what should be where in the curriculum and how it should be valued' (Baynham, 2000: 18). As I have already said, there is no need for you to seek membership of the 'Education Club', but neither is it in your interest to dismiss potentially useful concepts as 'jargon'. These concepts can help you to gain a more scholarly and analytical understanding of issues in your teaching. If the meaning and application of these concepts are not clear to you, you have every right to ask for clarification.

Moreover, all disciplines develop distinctive ways of doing their disciplinary business. It is therefore not surprising that there are distinctive codes to be used in the HES subject area for conducting what might be called *educational work*. For example, you may have noticed that educationists encourage lecturers to 'reflect' on their teaching. The term 'reflect' is a key piece of educational code, which stands for a complex (but not always precisely defined) process of professional learning through self-examination and experience (see Moon, 1999a). Here is another example: educationists often use terms such as 'unpack' and 'deconstruct', and even 'interrogate' and 'problematize', as in 'Let's take a minute to *unpack* this notion of key skills', or 'Can we try to *deconstruct* these concepts of deep and surface learning?'. Education has borrowed these terms from other disciplines in the humanities and social sciences, and uses them to mean 'critique' or 'analyse' or 'not take for granted'. Here again, these terms are important parts of educational code, and stand for complex ways of doing disciplinary work.

A high premium is placed in contemporary higher education studies on challenging orthodox ideas, on uncovering the sometimes hidden values, assumptions and ideologies that underlie dominant or apparently 'common sense' ideas. This kind of endless questioning can be exasperating for newcomers, who naturally want to find a few stable ideas to hang onto, at least until they have become accustomed to the new theoretical landscape.

Nevertheless, it is important for newcomers to be alert to core elements of educational code, to try to discover both their meanings and their significance early on, and indeed to challenge them (or even *interrogate* them!) in discussion and written work.

Writing about teaching

In the following sections, I set out what I think are three essential elements of the writing that lecturers are required to do on HE lecturer development courses: *criticality, reflectivity* and *praxis*. These are fine examples of educational jargon in themselves, and I will explain what I mean by them in the sections that follow. All three of these elements usually appear, in some form or another, in all the programmes on which I have taught or that I have investigated in my research for this chapter. I will look at each of these elements in turn, and explain what they demand of the writer, why they are considered important and how you might approach them with skill and confidence.

Criticality

HE lecturer development courses expect participants to become conversant with the main ideas in this field, but to do so with a *critical* orientation. I alluded to this in my earlier discussion of distinctive ways of knowing within HES. All academic disciplines have developed notions of 'criticality' (though not all refer to it this way) and have elevated it to an exalted position. Indeed 'being critical' is often used as the hallmark of academic rigour, and as a way of distinguishing good work from poor work, or one level of study from another. You are no doubt keenly aware of the way your own discipline interprets this quality, and you may well regularly refer to it yourself in your feedback to students on their written work.

In HES, as in most of the social sciences, 'criticality' is understood (and valued) as *a distinctive orientation to ideas and approaches*. It is fair to say, as we often do, that being critical involves moving beyond description, but this is easier said than done. We often find that lecturers writing in this area for the first time assume that 'being critical' is the same as 'criticizing'. They assume that they are expected to find as many reasons as possible to rubbish the authors they are reading. You may find that the HE texts you read are difficult enough to understand, let alone criticize. You may also find that the arguments in these texts are often so convincingly made that you agree with them, and therefore have no wish to criticize them. This experience may mirror that of many of your own students.

In many ways, therefore, this key term '*critical*' is an unfortunate one, since its meaning in an academic setting differs in certain important respects from its more common sense meaning, which is 'finding fault'. In fact it is perfectly possible for you to *be critical* even if you agree wholeheartedly with the authors in question. There are parallels here with the term *literary criticism*, which is an activity that scholars of literature engage in. When such scholars engage in *criticism* they are not 'finding fault' with Shakespeare, or T.S. Eliot, or James Joyce. They are trying to bring new insight to bear on the text. Broadly speaking, that is what the course team have in mind when they encourage you to *be critical*. Perhaps *critique* would be a more apt term.

Imagine for a moment that you are writing a section of your coursework in an effort to meet the following instruction (taken from a course handbook):

> Start by reading Alan Rogers (2002) 'The Nature of Learning' (Chapter 4) in *Teaching Adults* (3rd edition), and then research wider sources of literature on theories of learning. From this research, select theories of learning which you consider relevant to your own teaching situation. Summarise and *critically appraise* [my italics] these theories and comment on where you stand in relation to these ideas in terms of your current thinking. Illustrate your answer with references to literature and examples from your own and colleagues' practice and/or your own experiences as a student. Identify areas/issues that you intend to research further.

Let us say that you have researched four different theories of learning, and you wish to show in your writing that you have indeed 'critically appraised' them. One way to do this would be to write two or three paragraphs on each theory, summarizing the main points, and presenting them as a series of summaries. Many educationists (along with specialists in other subjects) would call this approach *descriptive*, and they would consider it to be a fairly rudimentary approach to handling the four theories. Alternatively, you could discuss what you feel are the important and relevant ideas within these theories. This would demonstrate that you had gained a good understanding of what you had read, in that you were able to *review* the texts in your own words and not just describe them.

However, in order to *be critical* you would need to attempt one or more of the following:

- Compare and contrast the theories with each other. What ideas do the authors seem to share, even if they do not necessarily appear to agree? What are the main differences between the theories, either in their substance, or in the methods used, or in other respects?
- Distil from the theories a few themes, and then write about each of the themes, drawing on aspects of the theories as appropriate.
- Discuss what you feel are some of the assumptions underlying the theories. What appear to be the values, or the philosophies, which the authors adhere to – whether or not they make these explicit?

- Discuss what you feel are some of the wider ideas that might have influenced the authors. The authors may take for granted that you will recognize 'where they are coming from' in terms of academic schools of thought, and will therefore not be explicit about it
- Discuss connections, and possibly differences, between the theories you are *criticizing* and other readings in the course, even though these other readings may not appear to relate directly to the topic you are addressing
- Discuss the methods by which the authors seemed to arrive at their conclusions. For example, are their ideas firmly based on evidence – either from practical research or from a balanced review of the literature?

Any of these approaches, if carried out effectively, would demonstrate that you had moved beyond a basic understanding of the material you had read to achieve a *critical* understanding.

The additional difficulty is that individual educationists differ in their interpretation of the meaning of *critical* as it relates to ways of handling material in a written assignment, and in the way they expect students to demonstrate an ability to *be critical* in their writing. You will therefore need to be sensitive to these differences. If members of the programme team do not offer you their perspective on this and other key terms, you should initiate a discussion about such issues, and ask to see examples of such writing.

Reflectivity

The terms 'reflection' and 'reflective practice' are key pieces of educational code. One reason for this is a growing recognition of the important relationship between self-awareness and learning, and between personal values and professional practices. This principle is well established in many practice-based subjects, where students are encouraged throughout their courses to record and analyse aspects of their development as professionals, and it is increasingly a feature of many other subjects. You may therefore already have experience of facilitating reflection and reflective writing with your own students.

However, the benefits of reflective practice may not be apparent if you have not encountered this way of working before. Indeed, if you work in a subject area that does not have a tradition of reflective practice or reflective learning it might seem strange, if not downright bizarre, to be expected to focus so intently and explicitly on yourself in your writing for your lecturer development programme. Even using the first-person singular ('I') will seem odd – let alone placing yourself at the heart of the text. You will understandably wonder why you need to engage in such an introspective process, and how such a personal writing style can still be *scholarly*.

The philosophy of reflective practice is based on the idea that *personal* effectiveness is an essential component of *professional* effectiveness. This philosophy challenges more traditional notions of what it means to be a teacher, which emphasize the teacher's knowledge of their subject and hardly acknowledge the role of the 'person' in teaching. The various activities and processes associated with reflective practice have been devised to help us gain greater awareness and understanding of our 'selves' as professional tools. They help us to understand how and why we act, respond and feel the way we do in different work situations.

That said, it could also be argued that this emphasis on reflection in lecturer development is, at least in part, a symptom of a wider fashion in contemporary Western culture for personal disclosure – a confessional disposition – and I have some sympathy for that argument. And of course it is probably inevitable that reflective styles of writing are more problematical when they are assessed for credit towards qualifications and awards, than when they are used for private purposes. Nevertheless, I would strongly urge you to accept the premise, at the outset of your course, that reflection is a powerful tool for professional learning and development, and that reflective writing can facilitate this process. By the same token, I accept that reflective styles of writing do not come naturally to everyone. The following points are offered in the spirit of helping you to write reflectively in a way that is both beneficial for you personally and also 'acceptable' for your coursework.

Lecturer development courses vary considerably in the way they expect participants to write about reflection. You would therefore do well to inspect course documents, and possibly discuss the issue with the course team, in order to clarify their precise position. For example, some programmes place a premium on participants' knowledge *about* reflection – that is, 'reflection' and 'reflective practice' are seen as substantive topics of study in their own right, presumably based on the premise that an understanding of the rationale for reflective practice is an important foundation for the practical processes involved. Here are two approaches to this issue, taken from course documents:

Start by surveying some of the literature on reflection and reflective practice. Write a commentary on what you understand by these terms and your views on becoming a 'reflective practitioner'.

… it's worth acknowledging that there is no necessary relationship between developing the habits of a reflective practitioner on the one hand, and gaining an understanding of the concept of the reflective practitioner on the other hand. It is perfectly possible to acquire these habits without having studied their intellectual origins in depth. However, it is important to be able to have a personal rationale for engaging in reflective practice.

> For many people, it is valuable to be introduced to some of the
> theoretical ideas underlying the practice as part of this process of
> developing that rationale.

It is almost certainly the case that most lecturer development programmes
aim to help participants to develop the 'habits of a reflective practitioner',
whether or not they place emphasis upon knowledge *about* reflective
practice, but it is worth scrutinizing your programme to establish where it is
positioned along this continuum.

Lecturer development programmes also vary in the way they view *the
actual processes of writing* with respect to reflection. Certainly most programmes expect participating lecturers to describe the processes of reflection in which they have engaged during the course, including changes to
their thinking and their practice. In this sense, the writing is seen as a
medium for reporting acts of reflection. However, many programmes also
see the writing process itself as an integral part of reflective practice, in that
it provides a tool that directly facilitates reflection. This is hardly surprising,
since writing is an extremely effective process by which we are able to make
explicit, and externalize, and record, a reflective process that might otherwise be implicit, internal and ephemeral. This is why many programmes
encourage participants to maintain some form of reflective journal
throughout the course – not merely to create a record of learning and
development, but to establish a habit of using writing as a tool with which to
reflect. One programme advises participants:

> We advise you to keep a 'learning journal' for the —— programme.
> This is a way of 'thinking on the page' – using writing to formulate and
> develop your ideas in your own way. A learning journal is a regular,
> informal and relatively personal kind of writing that can be quite
> provisional and can make the process of learning visible. It is quite
> different from the kind of academic writing that is read and sometimes
> assessed as a final product.

You can see from this excerpt from one handbook that this course team –
like many course teams – believe that the actual process of reflective writing
bestows valuable developmental benefits. In my experience many participants find that the process of writing does help them to develop and
consolidate their thinking, even if they had to work hard at it initially. There
are useful resources available, which provide more detail on the theory and
practice of reflective writing (Moon, 1999b; Bolton, 2005).

As in all these matters, the more precisely you are able to identify the
approach to reflection and reflective writing advocated by your programme,
the more effectively you will be able to work within it.

Praxis

'Praxis' means linking theory and practice. 'Praxis' captures the essence of my third element of writing within HE lecturer development programmes – that is, the expectation that participants will demonstrate through their writing that they are able to use conceptual ideas to gain a deeper understanding of (and possibly change) their teaching and, inversely, that they are able to use their experience of teaching to evaluate conceptual ideas. In using the term 'praxis' I am drawing on the work of Paulo Freire (1972) and others associated with what is known as 'critical pedagogy', where theory and practice are integrated in order to effect *action* and *change.*

While 'criticality' and 'reflectivity' can be difficult for course participants to demonstrate in writing, 'praxis' proves even more difficult for many lecturers. This is because it requires not only an effective command of the first two, but also an ability to integrate them. Yet, from the point of view of the programme organizers, it is only really through such integration that the programme's overall objectives can be achieved – that is, helping HE lecturers to become both scholarly and self-aware, capable of renewing their practice in the light of both conceptual ideas and changing circumstances and experience.

Consider the following excerpt from the specification for coursework, taken from a course handbook:

> Then *reflect* on [a number of teaching sessions observed by colleagues]. Briefly describe these sessions and then, with reference to the literature on teaching and learning and the feedback you received from your tutors, discuss how the sessions contributed to the progression and development of your professional practice. *Critique* how you tackled some issues of equal opportunities and student diversity in these sessions and how you could develop this aspect of your practice. [my emphasis]

This specification contains indicators that the writer is expected to respond with both 'reflectivity' and 'criticality' (see my italics). In addition, however, the instruction to describe teaching sessions 'with reference to the literature on teaching and learning', and to 'discuss how the sessions contributed to the progression and development of your professional practice' are calls for 'praxis'. Writing for this coursework is expected to bring theory and practice together in order to account for the writer's changing practice.

But how to do this? Attempts to fulfil this kind of requirement often fall into one of two traps (just as your students probably do). Writers attempt to show they are aware of the theoretical significance of an aspect of their practice by inserting one or two references to 'the literature' after a description of a teaching event: e.g. 'In this way I was encouraging my students to become deep learners (Marton and Säljö, 1997)'. Or they attempt to show that they understand the practical implications of a complex conceptual idea by providing a brief anecdotal example from their practice: e.g. 'I regularly practise Constructivism with my second-year undergraduate students by asking them open-ended questions in seminar sessions'. Neither of these examples demonstrates that the writer has a full grasp of the concepts in question; nor have they spelled out the linkage between the concept and the practice. In order for a participant on a lecturer development programme to fulfil the praxis element they would need to develop their ideas more fully and more explicitly.

I have made up the example below in an attempt to illustrate what I think the essential elements of 'praxis' are:

There was a real buzz yesterday in my seminar session with second-years doing the 'Methods of Sociological Enquiry' module. There was a danger, of course, that the topic I'd given them to analyse (the French government's policy on the wearing of the hijab in schools) would simply provoke emotive debate, and that they would lose sight of the important academic parts of the task. Sure, there was lots of debate. But I was so pleased to see them using key sociological ideas and methods to structure their thinking. Each of the groups came up with impressive analyses of the relationship between gender, faith and schooling, preserving the complexities and messiness of those relationships. They even produced outlines of how they would research the impact of the policy, using both qualitative and quantitative approaches. I guess I have to take some of the credit for this! I set up the activity very carefully, with a sequence of steps for the discussion that I hoped would take them from their initial personal position to a more 'open' or 'research minded' perspective. And the group work I've done with them in previous sessions paid off, because the 'ground rules' we established at the start of the semester had become second nature to them. I remember David Jaques and Gilly Salmon (2007) talking about how groups get established, and the factors that contribute to their success. As a sociologist I'd want to be a bit more robust than Jacques and Salmon about the 'outside' factors that help to determine group behaviour, and not limit myself to the immediate social-psychological aspects. Nevertheless, they definitely alerted me to the need for really careful planning of group activities and group membership, including the allocation of roles within groups.

For quite a few of them, this was the first time I have observed them 'talking like sociologists'. Etienne Wenger (1998) has this idea of 'communities of practice', and I can see that the sociology 'club' might be an example of this, though I think the kinds of settings Wenger looked at are quite different from an academic subject like sociology, especially when most undergraduate students don't (shouldn't!) aspire to become professional academics. Nevertheless, I'm sure that part of what 'clicks' for those students who 'get it' (usually sometime in their second year) is an element of moving into full and confident participation in the culture of sociology, and language/jargon is important for this.

But the most striking thing was the way almost all the students were demonstrating a 'constructed' (Biggs and Tang, 2007) understanding of key sociological ideas by the end of the session. I'm really excited by the idea of Social Constructivism, because it helps me to understand why these kinds of activities have the potential to produce such genuinely thrilling results. I think the key to this was the combination of social/collaborative work and a well organised sequence of activities. It gives me an important role that isn't just the provider of facts.

My action points for the future, based on this modest success are:

• I needn't be too concerned about choosing provocative or controversial issues as the focus for work in class. If anything, this was part of why the session worked so well
• At the same time, I need to be as mindful as I can of the sensitivities of individual students in relation to the topic at hand. Despite my best efforts, I was unable to get a sense of how two or three of the quieter students were responding, and it's possible they felt threatened by the dominant 'secular/feminist' flavour of the discussion
• I need to draw out the link between these kinds of discussions and their forthcoming project work much more explicitly and practically
• I need to go beyond the 'buzz' if I am to make sound judgements about what is actually being learned in these sessions, and who is being left behind.

Even though this example of an entry in a reflective journal is a fictitious one, you can see that it contains aspects of 'praxis', in that the 'author' uses conceptual ideas as tools for deepening their understanding of a specific practical experience, and inversely uses their analysis of an incident from their practice to clarify their understanding of the concepts. There is also a clear element of planning for future action and change.

Conclusion

My intention in this chapter was to increase readers' sensitivity to the professional and disciplinary culture encoded in the writing requirements of lecturer development programmes. This will allow lecturers to engage with those requirements from a position of knowledge and confidence, and to use their experience of writing to attain a scholarly orientation to their role. Lecturers may even feel moved to question the taken-for-granted assumptions underlying some of the practices in these programmes, and to work constructively and collaboratively with programme teams to bring the writing requirements into alignment with shared objectives.

LIBRARY, UNIVERSITY OF CHESTER

5

Resources on higher education teaching and learning

Helen Fallon

Introduction

While lecturers and researchers know the literature of their disciplines, they may be less familiar with the literature of the scholarship of teaching and learning, either related to their disciplines or indeed the generic literature. Rapid growth in information about effective and innovative teaching, learning and assessment strategies and other aspects of teaching and learning, alongside the increasing proliferation of electronic sources, initially present challenges when searching for information. In addition, lecturers are interested in selecting literature that is research-informed, as in their own disciplines, but may be less sure of how to assess it.

This chapter identifies and describes key information sources for information relating to the scholarship of teaching and learning in higher education, including books, journals, databases, and websites of professional organizations and associations. It includes tips on effective searching of the various information sources.

Lecturers starting to teach often look for a textbook or handbook that will give them initial guidance on how to teach effectively. This chapter opens with details of popular texts often used on courses for new lecturers. This is followed by details of databases that are useful for sourcing peer-reviewed journal articles on teaching and learning. Specific journal titles are then given, followed by useful websites.

While many sources are referred to and examples of search topics given, the aim is to outline principles that will have applicability across disciplines. This chapter provides a starting point for new lecturers coming to the literature of teaching and learning for the first time. It stresses the importance of working with librarians in order to ensure you have access to the most relevant material for developing your teaching. Librarians can advise on new information resources and other relevant library service developments on an ongoing basis. Through these various sources, including the websites, lecturers can then create their own links, alerts and networks for keeping up to date with new material and following up on their own interests.

Textbooks and handbooks

Many of the following titles provide a useful starting point for new lecturers. Those who are interested in developing their teaching further, can consult the Open University Press/Society for Research into Higher Education (SRHE) publications list, which can be accessed via www.srhe.ac.uk. This list includes many more specialized books on various aspects of teaching and learning in higher education, written in a style that combines research with practice relevance. These are useful in exploring aspects of teaching and learning, developing practice in specific areas and higher education policy. Extensive bibliographies are provided with Open University Press/SRHE titles, offering directions for further reading. Other publishers in the field include Elsevier, Kogan Page, Routledge/Falmer, Sage, Taylor & Francis and Oxford University Press. These publishers' web sites provide further material and routes of inquiry for lecturers.

Teaching for Quality Learning at University: What the Student Does by John Biggs (2003) gives a theoretical framework and practical strategies for aligning teaching practice with assessment practice. It includes chapters on large class teaching, teaching international students and using educational technology and assessment. Fry et al.'s (2008) *A Handbook for Teaching and Learning in Higher Education* considers theories of teaching and learning and presents case studies illustrating good practice. Parts one and two of the handbook are generic, while part three offers discipline-specific examples in medicine, business and the humanities. Phil Race's (2001) *The Lecturer's Toolkit: A Practical Guide to Learning* offers accessible advice and useful tips on learning styles, assessment, lecturing, personal management skills, large and small group teaching, blended learning and peer observation and teaching. In *Being a Teacher in Higher Education*, Knight offers hundreds of practice suggestions and advice on planning, instruction, learning activities and assessment.

In addition to textbooks on teaching, new lecturers may need more detailed information on curriculum design and assessment strategies. Brown and Knight's (2007) *Assessing Learners in Higher Education* describes different forms of assessment and offers practical advice on how best to assess. They argue that the method of assessment determines the nature of what is taught, its content and how it is learned. They suggest that it is therefore necessary for lecturers to determine what they want to assess and the purpose of assessing the students' knowledge, before they decide how to assess their students. This book is useful both for newcomers to the topic of assessment and for those experienced in practice but limited in theoretical background.

Bryan and Clegg's (2007) *Innovative Assessment in Higher Education* presents case studies of assessment innovations in the context of the pedagogy of assessment innovation. Toohey's (1999) *Designing Courses for Higher Education* deals comprehensively with the course design process, encouraging lecturers to consider the development of the 'whole person'. Prosser and Trigwell's (1999) *Understanding Learning and Teaching* also emphasizes the need for lecturers to be aware of students' prior experiences, their perceptions of their current learning and teaching context, and their approaches to learning. They emphasize that the learning context needs to be constantly redefined.

Those interested in using reflective practice will find Cowan's (2006) *On Becoming an Innovative University Teacher: Reflection in Action* useful. It gives practical advice on helping students to become effective learners. Reflection and reflective practice are covered in detail, and a useful guide to finding other material on reflective practice is included. Brockbank and McGill's (2007) *Facilitating Reflective Learning in Higher Education* aims to help university and college teachers shift their emphasis from teaching to learning, for which the authors argue 'facilitation' is a key skill. The last section of the book gives examples of reflective practice in operation.

Technologies as tools for teaching and learning, including virtual learning environments (VLEs), are constantly developing. The effectiveness and value of different technologies and their application are explored in Laurillard's (2002) *Rethinking University Teaching*. Drawing on examples from the Open University, she provides a theoretical basis for designing and using learning technologies, underpinned by understanding of how students learn.

Routledge/Falmer publish *Giving a Lecture: From Presenting to Teaching* by Exley and Dennick (2004), a useful guide for the new lecturer or postgraduate teaching assistant, covering topics such as how a lecture can be used to support student learning, preparation and coping with nerves, effective ways to structure and organize material and aids. Written in an accessible style, *Learning to Teach in Higher Education* by Paul Ramsden (2003), also published by Routledge, aims to change how lecturers think about teaching. He proposes that in order to become a good teacher, you need to understand students' experiences of learning. From this model a set of principles for effective teaching in higher education is developed. Issues such as quality, standards and professional development are also addressed.

Boden's (2005) *Academic's Support Kit* and Morss and Murray's (2005) *Teaching at University: A Guide for Postgraduates and Researchers*, both published by Sage, will be of use to new lecturers and postgraduates students who are teaching their first course, or part of a course. A distinctive feature of *Teaching at University* is that it includes guidance at the end of every chapter on producing materials for a 'teaching portfolio'.

Other titles that may be of interest to both new and experienced lecturers, and to heads of department and experienced lecturers with responsibility for mentoring new lecturers, include Brookfield's (2005) *Discussion as a Way of Teaching: Tools and Techniques for University Teachers*; Canon and Newble's (2002) *Handbook for Teachers in Universities and Colleges: A Guide to Improving Teaching Methods*; Gibbs and Jenkins' (1992) *Teaching Large Classes in Higher Education* and McKeachie and Svinicki's (2006) *Teaching Tips: Strategies, Research and Theory for College and University Teachers*. Eggins and MacDonald's (2003) *The Scholarship of Academic Development* explores the development of a formal scholarship of teaching and learning and the development of teaching and learning centres.

To keep track of emerging publications, in order to develop or update this material, a search can be run on the database *Nielsen BookData Online*, which gives details of all English language books currently in print and includes details of contents and reviews, where available. Bibliographies in relevant books provide a gateway to additional titles. As new thinking on learning and teaching in higher education develops, more titles will be published. The resources listed above should act as a starting point.

Members of university libraries can access books that are not held in their university's library through an interlibrary loan system. Under the Society of College National and University Libraries (SCONUL) access scheme, academics and postgraduate researchers in the UK and Ireland, have various levels of access – frequently including borrowing – to the university libraries of the UK and Ireland. Further details, including participating libraries, are available at www.access.sconul.ac.uk/

Tight (2003) conducted an analysis of books that focus on higher education. His research focused on titles in the English language, published outside North America, that were in print in 2000. He identified 284 titles, published by eight presses: Open University Press (including linked publication with SRHE and McGraw-Hill), Kogan Page, Jessica Kingsley, Taylor & Francis, Ashgate, Elsevier, Cassell and Oxford University Press. His analysis showed that Open University Press has the biggest list in the field, accounting for 39 percent of titles, followed by Kogan Page with 22 percent. Jessica Kingsley, which has ceased publishing new books in its series on higher education, accounted for 17 percent of total titles, followed by Taylor and Francis with 9 percent. Ashgate and Elsevier accounted for 4 percent each, while Cassell and Oxford University Press accounted for 2 percent each.

Over half of the books in print in 2000 that Tight reviewed were published since 1997. Tight (2003: 56) estimated the annual output of new titles was between 40 and 50. From his research he drew attention to the following:

- The limited number of publishers involved in producing books based on higher education research, and the somewhat volatile nature of this business;

- The popularity of edited, as opposed to authored, books on higher education;
- The dominance of books focusing on course design and system policy;
- The dominance of books based primarily on documentary analysis;
- The strength of the 'how to' literature, as compared to the academic monograph, particularly in writing about teaching and learning and related topics;
- The focus of the majority of books on national, international or system levels;
- The emphasis on UK based authors, when compared to authors of journal articles; and
- The dispersion in involvement in higher education research amongst education, staff development, social sciences and other university departments and functions.

Tight's analysis serves as a useful starting point for the analysis of trends and themes in the literature on higher education.

Identifying databases

Databases can provide a useful gateway to the content of thousands of journals and conference literature. A database search is particularly useful if you want to find information on a particular topic, but do not know where it might have been covered in the journal literature. As in other disciplines, databases in higher education provide abstracting and indexing and, increasingly, fulltext of journal articles, conference papers and other information sources.

Major publishers of journals in the field of higher education such as Blackwell, Elsevier, Taylor and Francis and Sage offer online access, on a subscription basis, to their content via their websites. It is possible to search for both individual and comprehensive listing from a publisher in this way. Alerting services, offered by publishers, give the searcher customized updating of search results. These provide regular electronic notifications to a requestor's email address. Services available include newly published research, tables of contents of selected journals, citation alerts and other types of information based on user-specified criteria. Free registration is usually required.

In addition to individual publishers' databases, there are databases that bring together content from a variety of publishers. The top database in the area of teaching and learning in higher education is Academic Search Premier, which offers the full text of a large number of higher education titles, including those published by Blackwell, Routledge, Sage and Wiley. These publishers, while allowing their content to be included in the database, impose an embargo on the inclusion of full text for 12 to 18 months. The full text of more recent issues is available via the publisher's website.

One of the advantages to searching a large multi-disciplinary database like Academic Search Premier is that it pulls together, in one search, material from a wide range of journals and conferences. For example, a search on 'assessing student learning in Physics' yielded 15 articles from a variety of journals, including *Physics Teacher, Physics Education, British Journal of Educational Psychology, American Journal of Physics* and *Assessment Update*, in addition to conference papers from the American Institute of Physics (AIP). A search on 'problem-based learning in Nursing education', in addition to yielding results from a Nursing and Nursing education journals, produced articles from *Teaching in Higher Education, Change* and *Social Behavior & Personality*.

Academic Search Premier offers an alerting service. Searches can be saved and, through a 'run alert' feature, executed at periodic intervals, and additions to the database emailed to individuals. In addition to searches, the contents of specified journals can also be emailed, as can details of citations of particular articles. Search results can be exported directly, in a wide variety of citation styles, through bibliographic management software embedded in the database.

ERIC is a well established, non-commercial database produced by the Institute of Education Sciences (IEI) and the US Department of Education. It offers free access to over one million records from journals and other education-related materials. Most provide abstracts, with a limited number having fulltext. ERIC is also available on subscription as ERIC International. This includes Australian Education Index, which indexes articles from over 500 Australian and international journals, and British Education Index, which covers over 300 education journals published in the British Isles, along with reports and conference literature. An ERIC search on 'using technology in the teaching of History in higher education', yielded articles from a range of general higher education journals, the journal *History Teacher* and a range of reports, many of which are available in fulltext, free of charge. It is possible to set up an account in ERIC for regular email alerts of new content on a particular topic.

Web of Knowledge (Institute for Scientific Information) encompasses a number of databases including Social Science Citation Index, Arts and Humanities Citation Index and Science Citation Index. This is an abstracting, not full text, database. A search across all three databases on the scholarship of teaching and learning yielded 15 results from the following journals: *Academic Psychiatry, Academy of Management Learning and Education, American Journal of Pharmaceutical Education, Health Communication, Journal of Animal Science, Journal of Education Policy, Studies in Higher Education, Research in Higher Education, Review of Educational Research, Teaching in Higher Education* and *Teaching Sociology*. Web of Knowledge allows users to register for automatic updates to searches via email, to set up table of contents email alerts, and citation alerts, which notify the user by email when a particular article has been cited by a new article.

Articles on the scholarship of teaching and learning in a particular discipline will generally be included in the indexing of the literature of the discipline. If searching for information relating to engineering, subject-specific databases, such as Compendex and IEEE Xplore, should be consulted, in addition to education-related databases. A search on Compendex for 'assessment in engineering education', yielded a large number of conference papers and a number of articles from scientific journals.

A major source that gives access to over 14 million items, including journal articles is OAIster, available at www.oaister.org/. This open access database provides abstracts and/or fulltext of journal articles and other sources useful to the study of interest to the new lecturer. Content is made up of submissions to institutional repositories worldwide. Increasingly, academics are depositing copies of their journal articles in institutional repositories. These repositories are in turn being harvested, so that large databases of journal articles, theses and other resources are now available free of charge, to anyone with internet access.

Higher education journals

This section first gives details of journals that relate specifically to the scholarship of teaching and learning (SoTL). It then covers journals relating to SoTL in different disciplines, then general higher education journals that, while not dealing exclusively with SoTL, include material that will be of interest to the lecturer/student in the area.

Most of these journals have both print and online versions; a few are electronic only. While the majority are subscription-based, some are open access. In recent years there has been a growth in the number of peer-reviewed open access journals available free of charge via the Web. The *Directory of Open Access Journals* (*DOAJ*) at www.doaj.org contains a number of titles relating to higher education. Those most relevant to the area are listed below. This listing does not aim to be exhaustive, rather to act as a starting point for growing your awareness of useful journals in this area.

The following titles relate specifically to SoTL:

- *Assessment and Evaluation in Higher Education* (Routledge) covers all aspects of assessment and evaluation in higher education
- *New Directions for Teaching and Learning* (Wiley) offers ideas and techniques for improving teaching at higher level, based on practical experiences and on the latest findings of educational and psychological researchers

- *Teaching in Higher Education* (Routledge) addresses the roles of teaching, learning and the curriculum in higher education

These are available in print and electronic form, either via the publisher's website or through databases such as Academic Search Premier (Ebsco) and Informaworld (Taylor & Francis Group).

A number of electronic-only, peer-reviewed journals are now available free of charge via individual websites and through the Directory of Open Access Journals at www.doaj.org, including several relating to SoTL:

- *Higher Education Perspectives*
- *International Journal for the Scholarship of Teaching and Learning (IJ-SoTL).* Produced by the Center for Excellence in Teaching at Georgia Southern University, this journal publishes articles, essays and discussions on the scholarship of teaching and learning and its applications in higher education
- *International Journal of Teaching and Learning in Higher Education (IJTLHE).* Covers higher education pedagogy and the scholarship of teaching and learning
- *Journal of Online Learning and Teaching (JOLT)* addresses the use of multi-media resources in education
- *Journal of Scholarship of Teaching and Learning (JoSoTL).* Based at Indiana University, this title promotes theory-based SoTL investigations that are supported by evidence
- *Journal of University Teaching and Learning Practice (JUTLP).* Produced by the Centre for Educational Development and Interactive Resources (CEDIR), University of Wollongong, this title aims to bridge the gap between journals covering academic research and practical articles and opinions published elsewhere
- *Learning and Teaching in Higher Education (Lathe)* provides an international forum for scholarly debate related to learning, teaching and assessment in higher education.

There are also journals that deal with SoTL in the disciplines, the following being a selection:

- *Arts and Humanities in Higher Education* (Sage) covers various aspects of SoTL across different humanities disciplines
- *European Journal of Engineering Education* (Taylor & Francis) is the official journal of the European Society for Engineering Education
- *Journal of Architectural Education* (Blackwell)
- *Journal of Geography in Higher Education* (Routledge)
- *Journal of Nursing Scholarship* (Blackwell)
- *Medical Education* (Blackwell)
- *Teaching & Learning in Medicine* (Erlbaum)
- *Teaching and Learning in Nursing* (Elsevier)

- *Teaching Sociology* (*American Sociological Association*) covers all areas of teaching sociology at higher level. Occasionally, there are themed issues, such as 30(4), 2002, which is dedicated to issues in curriculum design and assessment in sociology
- *Teaching Theology and Religion* (Blackwell) concerns issues relating to teaching and learning in theology, including styles of learning, philosophy and theology of teaching, information technology and theological teaching
- *Teaching of Psychology* (Lawrence Erlbaum).

There are also general journals on higher education that include articles relevant to teaching practice:

- *Academe* (American Association of University Professors)
- *Active Learning in Higher Education* (Sage)
- *American Educational Research Journal* (Sage)
- *Australian Educational Researcher* (Australian Association of Research Education)
- *British Educational Research Journal* (Taylor & Francis)
- *British Journal of Educational Studies* (Blackwell)
- *British Journal of Educational Technology* (Blackwell)
- *Cambridge Journal of Education* (Routledge)
- *Chronicle of Higher Education* (Chronicle of Higher Education)
- *Educational Research* (Routledge)
- *Higher Education* (Springer)
- *Higher Education in Europe* (Routledge)
- *Higher Education Quarterly* (Blackwell)
- *Higher Education Research & Development* (Routledge)
- *Review of Higher Education* (Johns Hopkins University Press)
- *Research in Higher Education* (Springer)
- *Innovations in Education & Teaching International* (Routledge)
- *Innovative Higher Education* (Springer)
- *International Journal for Academic Development* (Routledge)
- *International Journal of Educational Research* (Elsevier)
- *Journal of Education for Teaching* (Routledge)
- *Journal of Further and Higher Education* (Routledge)
- *Journal of Philosophy of Education* (Blackwell)
- *Journal of Studies in International Education* (Sage)
- *New Directions for Higher Education* (Wiley)
- *Perspectives: Policy and Practice in Higher Education* (Taylor & Francis)
- *Studies in Higher Education* (Routledge).

Discipline-specific journals, may regularly or occasionally publish articles relating to teaching and learning within the discipline of the journal. Examples include an article on 'The Scholarship of Teaching and Learning in Textiles and Apparel' appearing in the *Clothing and Textiles Research Journal.*

Alerting services

As with the major databases listed in the previous section, the main journal publishers in the higher education field, including Wiley (now owners of Blackwell), Elsevier, Sage, Taylor and Francis (now encompassing Routledge and publishing journals on behalf of various organizations including the Society for Research in Higher Education), offer alerting services.

Tight (2003) gives an interesting content analysis of 17 peer-reviewed higher education journals, from seven different publishers during the year 2000. Taylor and Francis accounted for over half (nine) of the titles reviewed. Two other publishers, Blackwell and Kluwer, each published two of the titles under consideration. Fourteen of the 17 titles were published by publishers based in the UK. More than half of the 17 titles were linked with professional associations, societies or centres. The two dominant themes, accounting for nearly 100 articles each, (48%) of the 406 articles under review, were system policy and course design. Academic work (15%), the student experience (11%), institutional management (10%), quality (8%), teaching and learning (5.5%), and knowledge (2.5%) were the remaining topics covered in the literature under review.

Tight concluded that some journals appear more generic in their publication strategy than others, noting that the journal *Higher Education* was the only journal to have published at least one article on each of themes identified during 2000. One journal, *Higher Education Quarterly*, had published articles on seven of the eight themes. Four other titles, *Higher Education in Europe, Journal of Higher Education Policy and Management, Studies in Higher Education* and *Tertiary Education and Management*, had published articles on six of the themes. From this evidence, Tight infers that many higher education journals will publish articles on most aspects of higher education, provided they are of high quality.

However, most higher education journals tend to specialize. Systems policy dominated in the titles *Higher Education Policy, Higher Education Quarterly, Journal of Higher Education Policy and Management, Higher Education Management, Higher Education Review* and *Higher Education in Europe*. Course design received the most extensive coverage in *Active Learning in Higher Education, Assessment and Evaluation in Higher Education, Journal of Geography in Higher Education, Teaching in Higher Education, Higher Education Research and Development* and *Studies in Higher Education*. Three of the titles reviewed focus on other specialist themes: *International Journal of Academic Development* (academic work), *Quality in Higher Education* (quality) and *Tertiary Education and Management* (institutional management). Tight notes that only one of the journals reviewed, *Higher Education*, appears truly generic, in the sense that it had no dominant theme or issue in the articles published in 2000.

Higher education journals provide an opportunity to read the latest thinking on teaching and learning, while bibliographies in published articles offer opportunities to read further and to identify other relevant articles and journal titles. As lecturers become familiar with both generic and discipline-specific journals, they can draw up their own list of sources relevant to their needs. As these needs change over time, throughout the academic career cycle, they can access other journals and alerts.

Professional organizations and associations

The websites listed below act as a gateway to other useful sites and assist the new lecturer in making contacts both for professional support and for dissemination of ideas on best practice.

For the UK and Republic of Ireland higher education sectors, several bodies provide a range of formal and informal forms of support.

- All Ireland Society for Higher Education (AISHE): www.aishe.org/
  Promotes the professional recognition of teaching and learning in higher education through conferences, seminars, publications and an electronic discussion list.
- Higher Education Academy: www.heacademy.ac.uk
  Aims to help individuals and groups provide the best possible learning experience for their students. It is an independent organization funded by grants from the four UK funding bodies for higher education, institutional subscriptions and contract income for specific initiatives.
- ESCalate: escalate.ac.uk/
  Part of the Higher Education Academy. Acting as a subject centre for education, it provides a wide range of information resources, including extensive book reviews, a newsletter, details of various HE-related projects and a series of publications aimed at supporting teaching and learning and curriculum enhancement. Recent publications, available electronically, include Boyd et al.'s (2007) *Becoming a Teacher Educator: Guidelines for the Induction of Newly Appointed Lecturers in Initial Teacher Education;* Peake's (2006) *Observation of the Practice of Teaching* and Trahar's (2007) *Teaching and Learning: The International Higher Education Landscape – Some Theories and Working Practice.* ESCalate organizes conferences and other events. Papers from their events are available from the website.
- SEDA (Staff and Educational Development Association): www.seda.ac.uk/
  The professional association for staff and educational developers in the UK, SEDA promotes innovation and good practice in higher education. The website contains links to a large number of useful organizations.
- Society for Research into Higher Education (SRHE): www.srhe.ac.uk/
  Promotes debate and publication on issues of policy, on the organization and management of higher education institutions, and on the curriculum, teaching and learning methods.

Internationally, there is an equally wide range of bodies:

- American Association for Higher Education (AAHE): www.aahperd.org/ aahe/
- Australian Council for Educational Research (ACER): www.acer.edu.au/ Provides support to education policy makers and professional practitioners.
- Higher Education Research and Development Society of Australasia (HERSDA): www.herdsa.org.au
  Provides a scholarly society for those committed to the advancement of higher education and promotes the development of policy, practice and the study of teaching and learning.
- International Consortium for Educational Development (ICED): www.osds.uwa.edu.au/iced
  Promotes educational and academic development in higher education worldwide.

Many of these bodies hold international conferences, where new and experienced lecturers can share their innovations, discover others in the fields and elsewhere and network with those who are interested in SoTL in their disciplines.

Conclusion

There is a significant volume of high quality books, journals, databases and websites to help new lecturers develop their expertise in teaching and learning. This chapter is a starting point. They can add to the knowledge gathered here and from other sources by working with their subject librarians, who can provide ongoing support. They can help new lecturers find new resources as they become available.

6

Starting with the discipline

Jacqueline Potter

Observation demonstrates that teaching within the disciplines of higher education is as diverse as the disciplines themselves. Indeed, the predominant force shaping the quality of the teaching is the discipline being taught, rather than a defined set of characteristics or skills associated with a genericised concept of teaching. (Andresen, 2000: 146)

Introduction

When academics are asked what they do, many describe themselves in generic terms as university lecturers. The reflex is to follow up the initial question and ask in which subject or discipline, if this information is not automatically included. It is axiomatic in higher education that our discipline defines our own and others' understanding of us as researchers and as trained professionals. Our disciplinary contexts influence our world views and the world's views of us. Disciplinary belonging is considered a stronger affiliation for academics than loyalty to their employing institution (Becher and Trowler, 2001).

Discipline-specific approaches to teaching, and their implications for learning within the disciplines, have been areas of inquiry and research for several decades. Recent authors, such as Andresen (2000) and Kreber (2006) have, suggested that the nature of knowledge about teaching is partly discipline-specific and partly generic. However, educational development units that coordinate activities and programmes to develop individual and institutional scholarship in teaching and learning, have, until recently, been rather neglectful of the implications of the discipline backgrounds of participating academics. Prosser et al. (2006) drew attention to this in their review of the Higher Education Academy (HEA) UK accredited programmes in teaching, learning and academic practice. Identifying the problematic relationship between generic teaching and learning material and discipline-specific aspects of such courses was one of their key findings.

The global professionalization of higher education teaching has increased the number of academic staff systematically engaging with the scholarship of teaching and learning (SoTL). This can take the form of participation in institutionally based activities, such as accredited programmes or projects that encourage learning through inquiry. There is also an increasing number of national initiatives, including funded support, for SoTL. During a relatively short period of time, probably related to the increased scale of opportunity and activity to promote SoTL, it has become increasingly apparent that disciplinary backgrounds can and do influence views and approaches to SoTL.

This chapter explores the interactions and implications of disciplinary belonging and affiliation on individual engagement with and enactment of SoTL. It considers discipline-based academics as scholars in and of their subject. It explores the implications of engaging with SoTL both on an individual's development and teaching knowledge, skills and practices and on the 'home' disciplines.

The chapter is presented in three parts. The first presents perspectives on the interrelationship between individuals and disciplines as the sites of formation of academic scholarship, approaches to inquiry and professional practices. It includes a brief review of some of the most recent international research on approaches to teaching and learning within disciplines. The review includes examples of national practices that have embraced a discipline led approach to the scholarship of teaching and learning. The second part explores how individual academics engage with and enact SoTL within disciplinary contexts. It presents a range of case studies to illustrate variation in the motivations and approaches to teaching scholarship. It introduces a transdisciplinary model of teaching scholarship and compares the model's features to discipline research. In the third part, the interaction between home discipline affiliation and the development of a scholarly approach to teaching and learning are compared to models and experiences of interdisciplinary working.

Academic development and approaches to teaching and learning within the disciplines

Becher and Trowler (2001: 47) describe being a member of a disciplinary community as involving a 'sense of identity and personal commitment'. They contend that while it is an 'untidy level of analysis' (p. 64) the discipline, and within that, specialisms or fields of study, are useful constructs for identifying communities that share attitudes, values and cognitive styles. In turn, these shared features are mutually interdependent with the knowledge domain in which academics work. Adapting an earlier three-dimensional classification of disciplines by Biglan (1973), Becher (1989) used two dimensions to explore discipline differences: (1) the extent to which the discipline is concerned with application (pure-applied); and (2) the extent to which a paradigm exists (hard-soft). He used this to create a simplified classification of four categories: 'hard-pure', 'soft-pure', 'hard-applied' and 'soft-applied'. The classification and the categories are widely used in the international literature base and will feature in this chapter as we explore what is known of, and what might be implications of, disciplinary-belonging in SoTL.

Becher's (1989) initial work was a comprehensive ethnographic consideration of the role of discipline within academic careers and professional identity. It was based on a substantive literature review and interviews with more than 200 academics working in research-intensive institutions in the UK and the USA. One insight from that work was the different perceptions held within discipline communities of their and others' ways of working and practising. This included an 'intellectual pecking order' based on judgements of academic quality. These perceptions are related to a range of features that are particularly influenced by the extent to which the knowledge base is restricted by clear boundaries and is cumulative (hard) as compared to holistic and interpretive (soft) and the extent to which the knowledge base results in discovery and explanation (pure) or is functional or utilitarian (applied).

Using this model SoTL in higher education might be considered a specialism or field within education (a soft-applied discipline). Becher and Trowler have noted the 'susceptibility of … [higher education's] research agenda to dictation by non-academic interests' (2001: 179). Such perceptions may influence the interest and engagement of some disciplinary communities with SoTL. For example, current inquiry led by the University of Flinders, Australia, is scoping the level of participation of scientists (physicists, chemists, biologists and geologists) in teaching development courses. Initial findings indicate a lower rate of participation than from other disciplines.

The majority of Becher's interviewees focused the discussion on their research role rather than their teaching, which was not explicitly explored. Becher and Trowler (2001) concluded, largely from their review of the literature, that the links between pedagogy and the disciplines are important but underresearched. More recent literature has explored discipline approaches to teaching and learning.

For example, Donald (2002) synthesized 25 years of research on academics' approaches to structuring knowledge and learning tasks, looking at different levels of study, from a range of traditional disciplines across the sciences, social sciences and humanities. Working closely with academics from a small number of international élite universities, her work meticulously records the nature of concepts and knowledge structures in the study disciplines, how that knowledge is validated and the methods and modes of inquiry used. Donald articulates the relationships between faculty objectives and their approaches to enabling higher order learning. She identifies both distinctive challenges and approaches to teaching and learning in each discipline, related to its goals, and similarities in a range of higher order thinking skills that academics valued: 'Greatest agreement across the disciplines was found in the importance of students learning to identify the context and state assumptions, and change perspective, and their learning the selection, representation and synthesis process' (Donald, 2002: 283).

Similar work by Shulman (2005) extended the exploration of teaching and learning practices to a number of professions, including medical, legal and clerical programmes. Using detailed ethnographic approaches, Shulman set out to distinguish the signature pedagogies of these fields, and the characteristic forms of teaching and learning that organize how future practitioners are educated across the dimensions of thinking, performing and acting with professional integrity. If signature pedagogies exist, Shulman suggested, they would be replicated across institutes, as they provide early socialization into a field and comprise ritual teaching and learning acts, a moral dimension of beliefs about professional attitudes and values, as well as set of assumptions about how best to teach and learn. Examples cited include the case study method in law and bedside teaching in medicine. He described these as 'pedagogies of uncertainty': 'learning to deal with uncertainty models one of the most crucial aspects of professionalism, namely the ability to make judgments under uncertainty' (p. 57). Such pedagogies provide repeated opportunity for routine performance of complex behaviours in varying scenarios, with an element of public performance. In this context, novelty and variation in teaching and learning come from the subject matter itself rather than from modifications and changes to teaching approaches.

A contrasting approach by Lueddeke (2003) explored values and beliefs towards teaching and learning in four disciplines. He found that academics from technology and nursing were more likely than academics from business and social science to hold an information transfer/teaching focus orientation. Teaching orientation and discipline were also the main variables influencing individuals' approaches to SoTL. Using similar methods across a wider range of disciplines, Lindblom-Ylänne et al. (2006) also found scholars in hard disciplines more likely than colleagues from soft disciplines to take a teacher focused approach. However, they also found that teaching and learning approaches adopted by individuals were mutable and responsive to teaching contexts. This perhaps indicates the influence of disciplinary teaching practice norms across disciplines, for example, more use of large group lectures in many hard disciplines compared to seminars in soft disciplines.

These differences in beliefs, values and approaches to teaching and supporting learners associated with specific disciplines demand to be taken seriously, particularly if there are implications relating to 'what passes for scholarship' within and among disciplines (Andresen, 2000: 142). In many countries, at national level, the development of teaching scholarship within and for discipline communities has been an explicitly adopted approach. For example, in the UK, the Higher Education Academy (HEA) network of

24 Subject Centres, established in 1999, has generally been positively perceived by their discipline communities. The centres are currently piloting national subject profiles in order to map trends in the student learning experience within disciplines (HEA, 2007). The National Digital Learning Repository in Ireland is the only national teaching and learning development project across the higher education sector. It has developed around self-identified discipline-based communities of practice. In Scotland a research project researching undergraduate teaching and learning environments has developed understanding of teaching intentions and student learning as discipline-based 'ways of thinking and practicing' (for example, see Anderson and Day, 2005; Entwistle, 2005; McCune and Hounsell, 2005).

The perspective and understanding academics gain through engagement and extended inquiry within disciplines and disciplinary communities are significant in shaping individuals' knowledge and values and their approaches to inquiry. Equally, the impacts of individuals within the disciplines is similarly transformative on disciplinary practices. These impacts may be consciously understood by individuals, but often the implications of the discipline for academic formation and identity are poorly understood. It is often through the process of engaging with new scholarship, such as SoTL, that a deeper understanding of disciplinary norms, ways of knowing, thinking and practising become apparent.

Lettuca (2005) argues that although disciplinary differences are useful, particularly in identifying typical ways of thinking, individuals within disciplines will have their 'unique constellations of theoretical choices, epistemological commitments, and beliefs about what is important to study and how to study it' (p. 20). This individual experience and practice within disciplines, as researchers and scholars of teaching and learning, is considered in the next section.

Disciplines and the scholarship of teaching and learning

The initial appointment and subsequent career progression of most academics is still largely based on their research contribution to the scholarship and development of their subject specialism or discipline. Within a discipline, academic success is usually measured by a small number of criteria, such as the award of competitive grant funds, awards and positions of esteem within the discipline community and the number and significance of peer-reviewed publications. Common among the criteria, is the sense of discipline validation of the value and worth of the research endeavor. Despite widespread discussion and calls for a more balanced approach to appointment and promotion, both are often weighted in favour of prior research success. Academics experience their growth and development as discipline-based researchers as developing confidence, becoming recognized for their contribution, becoming more productive and developing more sophistication in their thinking and working as researchers (Åkerlind, 2008).

In the context of developing as scholars of teaching and learning, academics develop an inquiry-based approach to pedagogic problem-solving and discovery, linking their experience-based knowledge to the wider theoretical and generic knowledge base and remaining open to dialogue and critique in their professional development. Models vary, but Andresen's (2000) model, based on a concept of a scholar-teacher – as one who knows, from within the field or discipline, what it means to teach and learn the discipline knowledge – is relevant here. His model for teaching scholarship has three elements: (1) critical reflectivity as a habit of mind; (2) scrutiny by peers as a modus operandi; and (3) inquiry as a motivation or device. In turn, these three elements are considered in relation to academic research within disciplines.

The generic discourse on teaching and learning can be an entirely new and alien field of scholarship and research, and it can be discordant with experience gained in a particular discipline or department. Creating meaningful links between generic discourse and teaching and learning as experienced within discipline contexts is a critical element of enabling SoTL to flourish in the disciplines. It requires deliberate support and development. In accredited teaching and learning programmes in the UK, Prosser et al.'s (2006) study found that the balance between generic knowledge and discipline specialist support for teaching and supporting learning was an area for improvement.

For academics engaging in SoTL, scrutiny by peers may be the most likely reference point to their discipline-based research. In structured courses, the peer group is likely to comprise individuals across disciplines within an institution. Interdisciplinary discourse is often valued for the breadth and variation of perspective it brings to bear on individual teaching scholarship, but is not entirely congruent with the conceptions of scrutiny by peers within disciplines. Healey (2000) suggested that geographers were likely to be more open to innovation than many other disciplines, but few geographers published the outcomes of their teaching inquiry. Like many disciplines, geography has a well established and well respected journal of international standing (*Journal of Geography in Higher Education*) that disseminates educational research within a higher education, discipline context. Even among winners of Australian national teaching awards, scrutiny by peers, in the context of teaching scholarship, is unlikely to be evidenced in publications: while award winners were research-active and productive in their disciplines, publication about teaching practices was rare (Halse et al., 2007).

While inquiry is a sufficiently broad term to be common across discipline research and teaching scholarship, forms of inquiry, in other words questions posed, methodologies and methods used vary considerably across disciplines. D'Andrea (2006) recommends that scholars of teaching and learning concentrate on clearly determining the initial question for any pedagogic inquiry. She advocates using known methods from discipline scholarship within pedagogic inquiry to make the 'challenge of choice' more feasible. She proposes that this would help to professionalize inquiry into higher education in the disciplines.

Clearly, the ways of experiencing and enacting the scholarship of teaching and learning are diverse: they are open to influence from disciplinary, institutional and individual perspectives. These influences become much clearer in specific settings, and five brief case study examples illustrate a range of motivations, drivers and approaches to teaching scholarship. The examples include team and individual practices, within a single discipline and crossing disciplines. They exemplify a range of scales of endeavour and of inquiry methods from within and outside discipline practice norms. The examples are not intended to be representative of SoTL. Instead, they aim to generate insights into how SoTL is enacted by discipline practitioners. They allow us to speculate that the discipline-based scholar-teacher, with a vested interest in the well being of the discipline and the students studying it, will be engaged in teaching scholarship at an ideological and value-driven level, using this to derive and determine foci and questions for inquiry.

For most, the discipline or specialism provides the lived-in context for acting out SoTL. It also provides a lens through which SoTL is viewed as a form of professional practice. Within the context of professional development through central institutional initiatives and development programmes, SoTL can also be perceived as another discipline, or specialism, to master as part of professional academic development linked to career progression.

The case study examples and the literature reviewed here suggest that affiliation to a discipline, knowledge and experience of its norms and values (whether tacit or explicit), can and do influence not only academics' conceptions of teaching and learning, but also the values they place on particular teaching, learning and assessment approaches. These in turn influence their behaviours both as teachers and as scholars of teaching and learning. In the following section, the application of ideas relating to the development of interdisciplinary study are developed and explored to see if they might shed light on how academics can and do integrate the SoTL within their disciplinary contexts.

An interdisciplinary approach to conceptualizing SoTL in the disciplines

Interdisciplinarity is broadly defined by the OECD (1972) as interactions among two or more different disciplines. It is distinguished as integrative and consultative, drawing on more than one body of knowledge. It can be enacted by individuals, who immerse themselves in learning a new discipline – its norms, knowledge base, cognitive style and social practices – and then adopt and adapt theoretical or methodological approaches from both in order to explore new questions or work with new tools and methods (Lettuca, 2002). It can also be the outcome of collaboration among individuals from different disciplinary backgrounds. In such instances, individuals usually retain commitment to their home discipline's paradigms or perspectives but, through the development of shared goals and mutual understanding, come to value and appreciate the contributions and perspectives offered by other disciplines (Amey and Brown, 2005).

Teaching scholarship requires academic staff to engage with a generic knowledge base of theory and research on higher education teaching and learning and relate this to their experience-based knowledge from teaching within a discipline. It requires academics to develop a critical stance to their practice, and may also lead them to question the generic knowledge and dogma, as illustrated in Case Study 1.

Case Study 1

A lecturer developed an interest in how students developed their understanding in the discipline. The lecturer started reading around learning theories, which further led to a raised awareness of the wider, political and social issues of teaching and learning approaches in higher education. He started to engage in discussion on this with colleagues. This led to a co-authored critique of the dominant, generic theory-based, curriculum models as detrimental to the teaching and learning goals of the discipline.

Academics are expected to open up their pedagogic practices to peer scrutiny as part of the 'disciplined inquiry' (Shulman, 2004: 277; referencing the earlier definitions of Cronbach and Suppes, 1969). This involves framing questions and identifying and selecting appropriate methods to answer them. It seems possible, therefore, that when a discipline-based scholar engages seriously with SoTL, they will be working in an interdisciplinary way.

Luedekke (2003: 217) suggests that 'advances in the scholarship of teaching will occur more readily if they are closely aligned to the conceptual structure and epistemology of the discipline'. Lettuca (2005) describes how academics doing interdisciplinary research and teaching had to overcome discipline-based differences in language and learn new ways of conceptualizing phenomena or enhancing their understanding of new methods of inquiry. For some, their learning expanded or complemented their existing practices or beliefs and connected them with new scholarly communities: these individuals found interdisciplinarity empowering. However, for others, interdisciplinary work posed a considerable challenge to their discipline-based beliefs. The case studies provide examples of both. Case Study 2 describes the application of scholarly inquiry into practice in a discipline by practitioners to explore the validity of their claims and beliefs.

Case Study 2

An external examiner questioned the validity of a department's approach to marking final-year dissertations. She was unhappy that the project supervisor's mark contributed to the grade, noting that supervisors had marked more leniently. The programme team defended their decision, based on their rigorously applied marking criteria and transparent moderation process using a second marker. Nevertheless, the external examiner noted her disquiet in her report, and the programme team were obliged to respond formally. A literature review failed to produce any evidence to support or refute the external's view. The programme team opted, for one year, to triple-mark each dissertation and to undertake a detailed comparison of marking between project supervisors and markers from cognate and disparate specialisms. They used the results to review their procedure.

By contrast, Case Study 3 is an empowering story about SoTL bringing scholars together to work across discipline boundaries on common issues.

Case Study 3

As part of an accredited course on teaching and learning a lecturer worked with five colleagues, all from other disciplines, to investigate academics' and first-year students' perceptions of curriculum and study skills. The work was linked to an institution-wide project on the first-year experience. The cross-disciplinary team devised, administered and analysed the output from a detailed survey instrument.

The interdisciplinarity of SoTL may offer an inclusive and tolerant perspective on teaching scholarship within and across disciplines. The discipline of education is characterized by its broad range of methodologies (D'Andrea, 2006) and its permeable boundaries and its openness to new researchers and research activity (Becher and Trowler, 2001). Shulman (2004: 279) contends that education is not a discipline, but a field of study where 'the perspectives and procedures of many disciplines can be brought to bear' and, indeed, the case studies show scholar-teachers using methods from their discipline and personal tool set (Case Study 4) or more widely sourced (Case Study 5).

Case Study 4

A lecturer teaching a large first-year lecture course elected to explore whether student learning was different for curriculum elements delivered by didactic methods or brief, interactive discussion or problem-solving methods. Appropriating a respected method from his home discipline, the randomized control trial, he found that an interactive teaching style had a weak but positive influence on learning. The work was published in an educational research journal.

Case study 5

A lecturer applied for grant funding to develop and evaluate an approach to improving academic writing skills. She invited students from across the school to attend a writing skills workshop and obtained copies of their draft writing prior to the workshop and compared this to work subsequently submitted for assessment. The workshop was well received by students, and the materials and techniques developed were shared with the institutional learning support service. All the students worked on their draft writing prior to submission. However, because an unfamiliar quantitative textual analysis method was used, it was not clear whether the quality of their work had improved or not.

Huber (2006) describes discipline methods as offering academics ways to undertake classroom scholarship, and D'Andrea (2006) has suggested that higher education inquiry may be professionalized by encouraging the use of known, disciplinary methods by teacher-scholars and sharing methods of inquiry across disciplines.

If, then, we embrace an interdisciplinary perspective to teaching scholarship, the disciplines themselves may benefit, as teachers form a more developed understanding of their disciplines (Andresen, 2000). For example, as they explore changes in knowledge practices within disciplines (Huber, 2006) they may increase their understanding of the strengths and weaknesses of discipline practice (Shulman, 2004). Disciplines can benefit when teacher-scholars interrogate disciplinary ways of working and practicing. This is one potential outcome of exposure to different epistemic and inquiry models from other disciplines, including the field of education. Finally, situating the discipline as the focus for teaching and learning scholarship potentially allows greater scope for individuals and communities of discipline-based scholars to develop their interest in scholarship through inquiry, with tangible benefits to learners and the discipline.

7

Beyond common sense: a practitioner's perspective

Matthew Alexander

Introduction

I completed my postgraduate diploma in advanced academic studies (an accredited course on teaching and learning in higher education) at the University of Strathclyde and was, as I saw it, entering a new phase in my career as an aspiring academic.

While working on my MPhil I attended a writer's retreat organized by the editor of this book who, coincidentally, had also delivered the first module in the diploma that I attended, on academic writing. Over dinner Rowena asked me what I had learned from the diploma. 'Well, I think [scholarship] is all about common sense, really', I said. Rather than rolling her eyes at this cliché, she countered with, 'really … why?' This chapter was conceived at that moment.

When I was asked to write this chapter I began to reflect on my experiences of studying, learning and reflecting about scholarship. What had I learned, and how did my approach to scholarship differ from my approach before the course? These and other questions are both addressed in this chapter. This reflects my own experience and, as such, is a positive account. I make no apologies for this.

The first, and possibly most important, point that I began to realize when I started to think about it is that the course was a means rather than an end. Courses in scholarship do not transform you into a good teacher, learner or researcher, in the same way that a medical degree does not make you a good doctor. What these courses aim to do is give you access to the most relevant skills and information to enable you to start, and continue, to learn about your own, and other, perceptions of scholarship and to be able to apply these within your own discipline.

In no way do I consider myself an expert in the realm of 'scholarship', and that is precisely why I was asked to write this chapter. Musings on the theory of scholarship need to be left to those with the knowledge and skills to be able to develop this vital aspect of higher education. However, it is useful to consider how scholarship is understood and utilized at the 'chalk face' of higher education. Given that, my frame of reference will not be a string of references to academic theory, other than that with which I engaged as a student in the advanced academic sudies course. To attempt to embellish this personal perspective with the weight of theory would not be doing justice to the purpose of this chapter. But first, to contextualize this chapter I will outline my own story in order to demonstrate how scholarship became part of my life in higher education.

Before I started the course I had been in charge of running a training restaurant in the Scottish Hotel School (an academic department at the University of Strathclyde) for nearly six years. It was a job I really enjoyed, providing both undergraduate and postgraduate students in the department with the skills and knowledge to become effective managers and operators whilst dealing with the day-to-day demands of a busy restaurant. As a graduate in hospitality management with previous aspirations to become a teacher this was, at that stage, my ideal job. After several years in this post a colleague and friend asked me one day what the next stage was in my career. After some prevarication on my part he placed a copy of the course outline for the postgraduate certificate/diploma in advanced academic studies in my mail tray. Signing up for the first module of that course was to prove a turning point in my career.

Over the next three years I changed jobs within the department – from food and beverage manager to teaching assistant, now teaching fellow – completed the postgraduate diploma, an MPhil in hospitality education and a postgraduate certificate in research methodology in business and management. I presented papers at three academic conferences and had a journal paper accepted. Currently, I am about to start a PhD and have three further journal papers either in the pipeline or under review.

This account is not an attempt to boast or advertise my skills but to suggest that without an understanding of scholarship I would not have realized my potential in higher education, something I am still coming to terms with. In the sections that follow, extracts from my writings for the diploma in advanced academic studies (shown in italics) demonstrate how I developed that understanding.

Studying 'scholarship' at graduate level

Starting my first module on the diploma was a nerve-wracking experience. The course (on academic writing) had around 16 'students' around a table. We introduced ourselves, and I learned that most of my fellow participants were in academic posts. At that time it was eight years since I had set foot in a classroom, and I was concerned that I had forgotten how to learn. That first module provided me with an important lesson about studying 'scholarship' at graduate level. My undergraduate 'sponge' approach of sitting back and absorbing knowledge was no longer appropriate. As my 'Learning, Teaching and Assessment' module journal noted, I realized that I had been a 'Robert' type of undergraduate (Biggs, 2003: 3):

> I was content to diligently record what I was told (when I attended) and regurgitate it in the appropriate format. This I did and scraped into my final year by the skin of my teeth. My problem was that I was content to engage with learning on a surface level without really trying to understand the field.

Clearly, this was no longer going to work, and I found myself putting some effort into my study. At this stage it was fairly minimal, if I am honest, but the important lesson was the concept of managing my own learning.

As the course progressed so did my level of engagement, along with the extent to which my own learning style improved. I was learning how to organize my thoughts and my writing and, more importantly, I was learning by engaging not only with the course but also with the participants. This was a hugely positive aspect of the course; sharing ideas and views with colleagues from a range of faculties and departments contributed to my overall learning experience.

Learning how to learn became both the subject and objective of my study, once again the course providing means rather than ends. On reflection, it was interesting to note how many of my participants (and myself, if I am honest) found it difficult not to slip back into undergraduate habits during the modules. We complained about the tutor, the lack of PowerPoint slides and the lack of direction over the assignments. Many of my fellow students were doing the course because it was stipulated in their contracts that they had to obtain the postgraduate certificate in order to pass their probationary lecturer period. This undoubtedly influenced some of their approaches to the courses. I, on the other hand, was doing the course on a voluntary basis, and by the time I reached the final module I had come to realize that what the tutors were looking for was a representation of my own learning construct, my perceptions of the aspect of scholarship in question, rather than for me to tell them what I thought they wanted to hear.

So what did I actually learn from the experience of studying scholarship at graduate level? The next part of the chapter presents, roughly in the form of a narrative with extracts from the coursework I completed on the diploma, my journey through the modules of the diploma.

Doing the accredited course

In chronological order, the modules I studied on the diploma were as follows:

- Academic Writing

- Supervising Postgraduate Research
- Learning, Teaching and Assessment in Higher Education
- Web-Based Teaching
- Professional Development Planning
- Developing an Accessible Curriculum
- Integrative Module.

These provided a diverse range of educational experiences and, from a personal perspective, educational challenges. Many of the courses ran concurrently, requiring a certain amount of multi-tasking to achieve success. Inadvertently, I stumbled across an ideal starting module for the diploma. The module on 'Academic Writing' provided skills and techniques that sustained and enhanced my academic output and still do today, as I noted in my final reflection on that module:

> Without this grounding in writing methods and techniques I would not have been able to produce this report in any kind of methodical way. My approach to all written work has changed fundamentally and I have tapped into personal resources I did not think I possessed. This project was written using generative writing, writing to prompts and other simple techniques that have allowed me (on my MPhil) to produce in one instance 4000 words in a day. ('Integrative Module' journal, 2006)

The 'Learning, Teaching and Assessment' module required us to conduct (through a combination of reflection and peer review) a wide-ranging analysis of our approaches to scholarship in specific classes we were teaching. I found this especially useful with regard to modes of teaching. In the following three examples my developmental stage is highlighted and then contextualized within large-scale teaching methods:

> Novice/Expert theory in teaching (Berliner 1989, cited in Kerrins and Cushing, 2000) suggests a five-stage theory of teaching development and the five stages are as follows:
>
> 1   Novice
> 2   Advanced Beginner – Development of both episodic and strategic knowledge
> 3   Competent Teacher – More conscious decisions are made about what is to be covered and more responsibility is taken on as a result
> 4   Proficient – Intuition and know-how have prominence
> 5   Expert – Have both an intuitive grasp of the situation and a non-analytic and non-deliberative sense of the appropriate response to be made
> (Adapted from Berliner 1989, cited in Kerrins and Cushing, 2000)

Upon reflection I would put myself somewhere around stage 3 of this model in that I feel more qualified to make decisions about content, delivery and learning outcomes without feeling the need to take advice. The model does suggest that experience in teaching is valuable to provide this 'episodic' knowledge and this certainly fits in with my own developmental experience. ('Learning, Teaching and Assessment' journal, 2005)

One of the more 'conscious decisions' taken as a result of this reflection was to consider further the activities I used to engage students in the learning environment:

I am not keen on the term lecture and have never just stood up and delivered material without seeking some kind of interaction or feedback from the students. Contact sessions should be a time to engage students on material already inputted through other means or to vary the type of input to keep concentration levels intact. The challenge is to take this environment and use it as a medium to encourage 'deep' learning. In terms of enriching the time spent in the 'lecture', Huxam (2005) advocates the use of 'interactive windows' which are 'opened within the lecture to allow the fresh air of discussion and thought' into the more serious atmosphere which can be created in the lecturing environment. Huxam's research tests the validity of interactive sessions with favourable results including popularity amongst students who favoured the interactive nature. ('Learning, Teaching and Assessment' journal, 2005)

My further observations on large-scale teaching considered coverage of material:

This is a practice which is not advocated in literature and Gardner (1993, cited in Biggs 2003: 46) stresses that the 'greatest enemy of understanding is coverage ... if you're determined to cover a lot of things; you are guaranteeing that most kids will not understand'. This has highlighted to me that my existing practices encourage surface learning. ('Learning, Teaching and Assessment' journal, 2005)

One of the most important aspects of studying courses within the diploma was that we were asked in every module to look at our practice through the lens of existing theory in the area. It was through this kind of reflexive process that I began to gain an understanding of scholarship and its importance in the activities I was undertaking on a daily basis. The following example comes from the 'Web-Based Teaching' module, where I was comparing elements of web-based material I had created with established theory on e-learning, in this case Salmon's (2003) five-stage model of teaching and learning online:

> THEORY: The socialisation process and components 'can gradually develop throughout the five stages, success comes with a strong foundation on stage two'. This stage is all about encouraging the students to communicate in a free and unconstrained environment and moderating in an encouraging and supportive manner. This stage can solicit responses from students who may otherwise have remained silent. The stage ends when students 'share a little of themselves online.' (Salmon, 2003: 34–37)
>
> PRACTICE: Both public and private discussion boards have been provided in the online content. A concern would be the propensity for students to take up the opportunity to socialise in this way. There perhaps needs to be some kind of gentle encouragement (in the form of a compulsory 'post') which may spark some further discussion. The private discussion where students can discuss their project work may be used more widely. ('Web-Based Teaching' module, 2005)

On a day-to-day level understanding scholarship is more than a simple application of theory. In my case scholarship was about building an understanding of my own behaviour within my own practice and giving consideration to how it could be improved/adapted:

> The 'Creating an Accessible Curriculum' module gave me the opportunity to take an in depth look at my own practice and make appropriate suggestions relating to improving practice in both general and accessible terms. One of the key learning outcomes of this class was the realisation that accessible teaching does not necessarily require a new or complex skill set. Accessible teaching is in many cases simply good teaching practice. ('Integrative Module' journal, 2006)

The true test of scholarship is how you apply your understanding in your teaching and learning practices. The following section outlines some of the ways in which scholarship has become embedded in my own practice.

Teaching students in ways that make them want to understand

This chapter was written during a writing day I organized for honours students in the department. During their induction programme I had previously delivered a one-hour session on writing, based on my experiences from the diploma and writing a thesis. The concepts I introduced to the students during that session, such as 'free writing' (Elbow, 1973), had been well received by the students to the extent that they wanted more writing practice. The writing day was then organized to give them a supportive and collective environment in which to progress their dissertations. As I write this, heads are down and fingers are flying over the keyboards.

Free writing (the act of writing on a particular subject, without stopping, for five minutes) has also found its way into undergraduate teaching at levels 1 and 2. I frequently ask students to free-write on an aspect of the topic we have been discussing in class. This may be linked to an assignment or exam, but it allows students, albeit briefly, to review and reflect on the material.

Use of reflection as a learning tool was a strong thread running through the diploma in three of the modules: 'Learning, Teaching and Assessment', 'Professional Development Planning' and the 'Integrative Module'. I have come to value highly the ability to be self-critical both within my personal and professional life. Reflection is a skill that develops over time (much like scholarship), and I incorporate this into my assessment at both levels, 1 and 2, where students are asked to reflect not only on their understanding of hospitality but also on their performance within a group assessment. I noted in my final reflection that:

> Perhaps the greatest benefit from the diploma has been from reflecting on my current practices and investigating changes and improvements that could be made. As Biggs (2003) states 'expert teachers continually reflect on how they might teach even better'. ('Integrative Module' journal, 2006)

The key benefit for me is the extent to which my practice in both small- and large-scale teaching methods has changed. The changes are too various to mention in this chapter, but principally an understanding of student learning methods and of how to enhance the delivery of classes has contributed to an improved experience for the students. I spend a great deal more time planning classes than I did pre-diploma, both at course level and individual lecture level. As a result, feedback from classes has improved and often highlights that lectures are well timed and slides are not skipped or missed out. I also make better use of alternative delivery methods in class, such as imagery, story telling and music to aid understanding and create more of Huxam's (2005) interactive windows to reinforce student understanding. My understanding of course design has allowed me to engage heavily with curriculum development at a departmental level and create new courses.

Part of the coursework for some of the modules on the diploma involved reflecting on scholarship within my own discipline, and in the next section I describe how good scholarship is mirrored, to an extent, by the theory from within my discipline of hospitality management.

Dealing with the 'customers'

I can imagine the impact this heading will have on some readers. The concept of students as customers is unpalatable and alien to many academics concerned about the increasing 'commoditization' of higher education. But please bear with me here. It is not my intention to make some impassioned argument about providing value for money etc., but rather to demonstrate how good scholarship can mean different things in different disciplines. Understanding how students construct (or are taught to construct) good practice in a particular discipline or subject area has led me to think in a different way about my approach to scholarship. Studying teaching and learning in higher education gives you the skills to engage with scholarship in a more reflective way, in this case to identify the links between my own and students' understandings.

Students in hospitality management learn to view the world through the lens of a transaction between host and guest. The experience of customers in the hospitality environment mirrors, to a certain extent, their own experiences as students. I want to present two models that I use with students. First, there are theoretical constructs that aid students' understanding of how a hospitality business can be viewed from a systems perspective. Second, there are service operations that attempt to maintain customer loyalty. I make a connection between these models in order to propose that personal understanding of scholarship comes not solely from engagement with specific academic theory but from contextualizing theories and concepts learned in a specific discipline. Post-diploma I started to view my teaching through the lens of models such as these and to consider these components in the context of my own practice. Figure 7.1 shows that the 'feedback' component is crucial to the hospitality business, as it allows it to learn about customer satisfaction and financial success or failure.

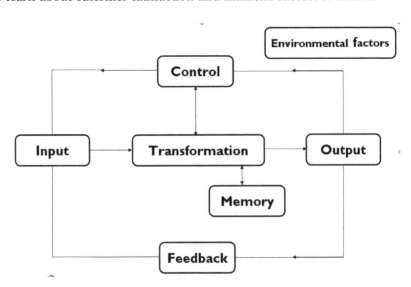

Figure 7.1 Systems model (adapted from Spears and Gregoire, 2006)

In my teaching, student feedback is essential for making continuous improvements to my teaching. However, feedback does not have to be expressed explicitly. Many times I have come out of a class thinking 'that was not a good lecture/tutorial' and reviewing the delivery method and thinking about changes I could make. In academic terms the 'control' component takes the form of class outlines and assessment mechanisms, providing a logical route through the learning experience for students, and a focus for tutors.

The 'memory' component of the model is also important in scholarship terms. Here I make reference to scholarship as something learned and improved upon. The more I teach, the more I learn about scholarship and the more I can improve upon my own practice and draw on my own experiences. 'Transformation' is the learning experience itself, whether small or large scale, and 'outputs' are the students' coursework. Figure 7.2 develops these connections between the scholarship of teaching and learning and my home discipline of hospitality management.

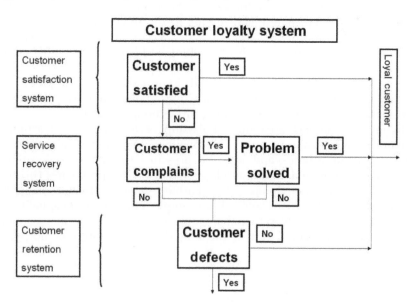

Figure 7.2 Customer loyalty model (adapted from Bateson and Hoffman, 1999)

In terms of customer loyalty, keeping students on board throughout the course of a class is often a challenging task, particularly if you are dealing with a large group of individuals. Maintaining customer loyalty in scholarship terms is about providing students with feedback and the opportunity to check their understanding of concepts throughout the class. Maintaining customer satisfaction is about being available to students, providing appropriate formative assessment and feedback. Service recovery is dealing with things that go wrong, students who do not understand, students who fail assignments, and retention in higher education means exactly the same thing as it does in hospitality. The idea is to keep students/customers on board and prevent them dropping out/defecting.

Scholarship can therefore be understood in different ways in different disciplines. To conclude this chapter I make some final connections between my own work on the course on teaching and learning in higher education and my career and, finally, I report on the texts that I found the most useful during my study of the scholarship of teaching and learning in higher education.

Making connections

So, this 'scholarship' thing – is it all about common sense, then? Well, not really, actually. Scholarship is a highly complex blend of generic and individual understanding of the activities associated with learning, teaching and assessment in higher education. Scholarship can be constructed in different ways, each, potentially, unique to the discipline, subject or individual. My study at diploma level only scratched the surface of the wealth of literature available on the study of teaching and learning in higher education, suggesting that engaging with scholarship does not necessarily mean you have to be an expert in that field. Experience on the diploma and further study have taught me that learning about scholarship involves a considerable commitment to learning throughout your career.

In my own subject area the scholarship of teaching and learning is debated heavily in the literature. Hospitality management has suffered by association with a past – and, arguably present – that is largely vocational. Academics in the field argue for adopting alternative approaches (Brotherton and Wood, 2000; Jones, 2004; Lashley, 2004; Lashley et al., 2007; Morrison and O'Gorman, 2007). For example, the study of hospitality as a phenomenon of society, rather than studying hospitality for management, suggests a fundamental shift in the underlying philosophy of hospitality education.

More critically, there is debate about how hospitality education at the higher education level is delivered. Critics argue that much hospitality education has an overly vocational purpose and that students need to engage with learning at higher, more reflective, levels in order to contribute more towards the subject area (and the industry) (Airey and Tribe, 2000; Tribe, 2002; Morrison and O'Mahony, 2003). These teaching and learning debates within the subject area directly impact on the scholarship and scholarly practice of those working within the discipline. An enhanced understanding of scholarship gained through formal study, such as the diploma I experienced, has certainly aided my understanding of these debates and, indeed, through my thesis and publications I am contributing towards them.

Learning about scholarship, as I have argued in this chapter, is very much an individual process. However, the following texts proved extremely useful to me throughout my diploma. Students are always looking for a 'catch all' text, and if I had to recommend one it would by Fry et al. (2008), which provides wide-ranging debate on scholarship in higher education. In terms of academic writing Murray (2006) remains a text that I return to again and again for guidance. Salmon (2003) was extremely valuable when setting up the now seemingly all-important online learning activities. These can aid other learners towards an enhanced understanding of scholarship. Believe me, it's a road worth travelling.

8

Evaluating teaching and learning: enhancing the scholarship of teaching by asking students what they are learning

Diana Kelly

Introduction

In higher education we sometimes pause at the end of a lecture and ask, 'Any questions?' or 'Is everything clear? It is not unusual, particularly in large classes, particularly if the lecture time is more or less up, for there to be no responses, and, as students leave the room we can be relatively satisfied that we at least allowed students the opportunity to ask questions. As there were no questions, it is possible to assume that the students must have understood the lecture. However, how do we really know what students are actually learning, particularly when they are in the process of learning something new? Lecturers are not mind readers. We need to check in with our students to find out what they are learning and what they do not understand fully and try to work out why.

Lecturers who care about what students are actually learning often find informal ways to ask students what they have learned. However, by systematically and thoughtfully asking students about their learning as a normal integrated part of a lecture, we can gain valuable feedback about gaps in their understanding of a specific topic. The goal for lecturers is to gain an understanding of what students know (and don't know) in order to make responsive changes in teaching and learning (Boston, 2002). To help us do this, there are specific strategies that use the principles of student-centred learning.

This chapter provides strategies to help lecturers determine what students have learned in in-class situations: lectures, labs, tutorials, etc. Using these in-class strategies, lecturers can monitor students' learning progress and address or review difficult topics.

In this process, students become more skilled at evaluating their own learning progress, an essential skill for lifelong learning. Lecturers learn whether or not the teaching and learning strategies are actually helping students to learn. This can stimulate greater creativity in teaching and greater responsiveness to learners, as lecturers seek new ways to help students understand particularly challenging concepts.

This chapter begins with background on the use of strategies to check on student learning in higher education, describes examples of six practical ways to implement these strategies in teaching and concludes with a discussion of how student feedback on their learning can help lecturers to improve their teaching.

Background

First, a note on terminology: the strategies for checking on student learning described in this chapter have been called classroom assessment techniques (CATs) in the literature of North American higher education. However, this name might be interpreted differently by those in other higher education cultures. In this context, 'assessment' does not mean graded exams, but rather a set of teaching strategies aimed at improving the quality of student learning. 'Classroom' does not refer to secondary school, but rather to in-class sessions (lectures, labs, tutorials) in higher education.

The literature on assessment includes distinctions between summative and formative assessments. Summative assessments refer to assessments occurring after the learning has taken place, such as end-of-year exams or projects that are graded to make a judgement about the extent and quality of learning demonstrated. Formative assessments generally involve providing feedback to students on work-in-progress, such as essays or projects, after students have learned enough about a topic to work on an essay or project. Although usually not graded, formative feedback from the lecturer or from peers (i.e. other students) is usually a critique of work that is advisory or evaluative.

In contrast, CATs are used at a very early stage in the learning process, when students are first learning about a new topic. CATs are anonymous and non-graded, mainly aimed at gathering feedback from a group of students about what they learned and what they find confusing about a topic. They are used to help students in the process of learning a new subject.

Research

CATs originated in the late 1980s in two well respected American universities: Harvard (Mosteller, 1989; Light, 1990; Roueche, 1993) and University of California at Berkeley (Cross, 1987; Cross and Angelo, 1988, 1993a; Cross and Steadman, 1996; Davis, 1999). Since the beginning, classroom research has been done in the way that K. Patricia Cross (1987) originally envisioned:

lecturers use CATs to systematically find out what and how well their students are learning and then use the results to improve their teaching practice. This fits with Boyer's (1990) definition of the scholarship of teaching, in that it encourages lecturers in higher education to research the teaching and learning in their disciplines.

Comprehensive studies have examined the effects of CATs on student learning (Angelo, 1991, 1998; Kelly, 1991, 1993; Cross and Steadman, 1996). Results indicate that CATs have a positive impact on student learning, including achieving deep learning and increased involvement in the learning process. However, the impact of these strategies might be greater if used in a cohort group in which students travelled through a programme together, with all the lecturers on their course using CATs routinely (Kelly, 1991, 1993).

CATs have also had a strong positive impact on the professional development of lecturers as teachers (Kelly, 1991, 1993). There is no question that classroom assessment has helped many lecturers to re-think how they teach their classes (Cross and Steadman, 1996; Kelly, 1991, 1993; College of Marin, 1990). This can result in rejuvenation among long-term lecturers and increased confidence among new lecturers.

Learning theory

The notion of checking on student learning using CATs supports a range of educational theories: constructivism, experiential learning, deep learning and adult learning theories. CATs encourage students to think about what and how they are learning, to construct their own knowledge, link their learning with their experiences, and move toward a self-directed approach to learning. As Jarvis et al. (1998) point out, learning is regarded as constructed by the learner rather than received from the teacher. When learning something new, students try to understand the new information as it relates to what they already know. For this reason, the learner's role is central.

Asking students what they learned in the very early stages gives them the opportunity to reflect upon their understanding of the new material they have just learned. It is possible that misunderstandings can occur at this early stage, or there might be confusion in the minds of the learners because what they have just learned does not 'fit' with their prior learning. Using CATs, a lecturer can quickly see how students have interpreted what they have learned, can assess whether or not corrective action is needed, and can decide what to do to help students learn.

Students go through developmental stages as they become more confident learners in the discipline. As students gain confidence, they can and should be less dependent on the lecturer and more dependent on their own abilities as learners, so that ultimately they become self-directed lifelong learners. As students develop the ability to self-assess their learning, they can monitor their learning progress. They can also actively construct their own learning in their responses to the CATs and in the discussion of feedback from the lecturer. As a result, it is not surprising that research into the use of CATs has indicated that these strategies help students to become more reflective and confident as learners (Cross and Steadman, 1996; Angelo, 1999).

Best practice in teaching and learning

In the 1980s a research project was set up by the American Association for Higher Education (AAHE) to summarize best practices in teaching and learning in higher education. The results of that research project were summarized in 'Seven Principles of Good Practice in Undergraduate Education' (Chickering and Gamson, 1987). That publication was based on results from many research projects into teaching and learning in higher education. Several years later, the AAHE Assessment Forum developed 'Nine Principles of Good Practice for the Assessment of Student Learning' (Astin et al., 1995). More recently, the Higher Education Academy Generic Centre in the UK published the following seven principles for good feedback practice:

1 Facilitates the development of self-assessment (reflection) in learning
2 Encourages teacher and peer dialogue around learning
3 Helps clarify what good performance is (goals, criteria, standards expected)
4 Provides opportunities to close the gap between current and desired performance
5 Delivers high quality information to students about their learning
6 Encourages positive motivational beliefs and self-esteem
7 Provides information to teachers that can be used to help shape the teaching.

(Juwah et al., 2004)

Most lecturers start using CATs because they want to find out what their students are learning. However, most continue with CATs because it stimulates creativity and helps them to find ways to improve their teaching. Feedback from students often provides lecturers with a stimulus to try new teaching methods, aimed at enhancing student learning.

Implementing CATs

CATs are systematic ongoing strategies for collecting student feedback about their learning which answer these questions:

1 What are students actually learning in my lecture/lab/tutorial?
2 How are the students progressing toward the learning objectives?
3 Where are they having difficulties in learning?

CATs allow lecturers to determine the learning progress of a group of students by means of anonymous written responses to questions posed by the lecturer. The emphasis is on what students are learning rather than on what the lecturer is doing. Some lecturers gather feedback in student surveys at the end of the year. Although this is helpful in planning the next year's class, it does not directly benefit those who are currently on the course. Using CATs the lecturer obtains feedback from students as often as every session, or at critical points in the term/semester.

Before starting to use CATs, it is important for lecturers to clarify their teaching goals, using the Teaching Goals Inventory (Cross and Angelo, 1993b). Learning objectives will flow from the teaching goals, and should be explicitly communicated to students (Sadler, 1989).

Examples of classroom assessment techniques

CATs may be used in any type of class session: lectures, laboratories, tutorials, seminars, etc. Some CATs are for individual students; others are for use with small groups. Some are designed to check students' immediate understanding; others are for checking application and critical thinking. The following are examples of CATs that may be used to enhance student learning (Cross and Angelo, 1993a).

The one-minute paper

This is often used at the end of a lecture to give students the opportunity to reflect upon what they learned. Their anonymous responses provide valuable feedback to the lecturer that may be used in planning the next class session. There are six main steps for a lecturer:

- *Step 1:* About five minutes before the end of a lecture, lab or tutorial, hand out small cards or half-sheets of paper to students and explain that you would like some anonymous feedback about what they have learned, so you may help them with their learning.
- *Step 2:* On one side of the card, ask them to answer a question about the session, such as, 'What was the most important thing you learned today about _____?' or 'List three new things you learned today about _____.' A specific content-centred question is most effective to provide a focus for students.

- *Step 3:* On the other side of the card, ask them to write any new questions they have as a result of the lecture/tutorial, or write questions about any areas they didn't understand fully.
- *Step 4:* Keep silent for at least two or three minutes while students are writing, allowing them time to think and formulate their responses. Then collect the cards.
- *Step 5:* Tally and analyse the responses. This usually takes about 30 seconds per card. The cards may be arranged into categories by types of answer. In very large lectures it is possible to get a good sense of the group by sampling rather than reading every response.
- *Step 6:* Plan to spend about five minutes at the beginning of the next session briefly summarizing the feedback, and addressing areas that were not understood.

The one-minute paper can also be used at the beginning of a class to ask students questions about a reading assignment or a project they are working on. One-minute papers have also been used in the middle of lectures to encourage students to reflect on a particular point that has been raised, or to check on their comprehension of a new concept. In these cases it may be more expedient to get immediate feedback by combining the one-minute paper with a 'think–pair–share' activity, in which students first write briefly, then they pair up and share what they have written for about two or three minutes, and then the lecturer calls on a few students to get a variety of responses to the one-minute paper. The lecturer can also collect the cards for review after class. This is an efficient way to gather quick feedback from students, even in very large lectures.

Background knowledge probe

The background knowledge probe allows lecturers to learn about students' prior knowledge or experience in the subject. It may sometimes take the form of a survey at the beginning of the course, but could also be used as new topics are introduced. This strategy is useful for lecturers to find out about the variation in backgrounds of a group of students. Their responses may also be used to measure the overall learning progress of the group at a later stage in the course. A background knowledge probe usually takes the form of a survey that might include the following areas:

- Educational or work-related background experience in the subject
- Motivations/reasons for studying the subject
- Expectations for this subject – what they hope to learn, and how it will help them to be successful in the course or programme
- Concerns or apprehensions about studying this subject (e.g. memorization, exam anxiety, essay writing, previous negative experiences in this subject, etc.).

Although asking about apprehensions may appear to be negative, in reality addressing these fears from the beginning is helpful to students (Kelly, 1993), particularly when they find out that others have the same concerns. This also lets students know that the lecturer wants to help students to overcome these fears.

Focused listing

A focused listing exercise can be used at any time to ask students to recall a set of terms, facts or concepts that they should know. Although this strategy might appear to be at the lowest level of Bloom's (1956) Taxonomy, it can be used to check on recall as well as understanding of terms, if they are particularly important for the topic of a lecture. Some lecturers have used a focused listing exercise at the beginning of a class session to measure students' recall of a reading assignment, and again at the end of the class session to see the extent to which their recall and understanding of terms have improved.

Directed paraphrase

This strategy is particularly useful in measuring students' levels of understanding of a set of procedures or methods to be followed, although it can also be used to check for students' understanding of complex concepts or theories. This assessment may be given as an assignment to be completed outside of class, or it may be done during a class session individually, in pairs or in small groups.

Students are asked to write an explanation of a concept or a set of instructions in their own words, as if writing for someone who is not on the course. This paraphrase provides a way for the student and the lecturer to assess the degree to which students have understood an important concept or procedure and to see if there are any gaps in their understanding.

Memory matrix

The memory matrix is helpful if students are asked to compare and contrast various items for a higher level analysis. A listing of items is provided by the lecturer down the left side of the matrix, and several key characteristics are listed across the top of the matrix. Students then fill in the blank boxes with their understanding of how the items are different. This method can be used to improve students' analysis of different types of cells in biology, different types of government structures, different types of economic theories or different authors of a particular literary genre. It helps students to construct their own knowledge for deep understanding. The memory matrix in Figure 8.1 shows how students might use this CAT to analyse the writing styles of several different authors of short stories.

Authors	characters	plot	perspective	setting
Author1				
Author 2				
Author 3				
Author 4				

Figure 8.1 Memory matrix

Process self-analysis

Students are asked to write down all of the steps they took in carrying out an assignment or project, and the length of time it took them to complete each step of the project. They then analyse how they did the work, and which areas they found most difficult or most time consuming. This pinpoints areas in which they may need more work to develop the skills needed for this type of project. Process self-analysis can be used with any type of assignment, including project work, individual essay writing or research work.

Common questions about implementation

Lecturers who want to begin using CATs often have questions regarding the details of implementation. Concerns are often expressed in the following areas:

- *How much time does it take?* The most common barrier to implementing these strategies is the perception among lecturers that they will take up too much time (Cross and Angelo, 1993a; Juwah et al., 2004). Lecture sessions are short, and lecturers are concerned that it is already difficult to find sufficient time to 'cover the content' without adding CATs. However, those who have used CATs find that they save time in lectures by focusing on areas of greatest importance for student understanding. In addition, they find that students take more responsibility for their own self-assessment of learning, which also saves time (Boud, 1986). Linking learning objectives to what students are learning makes it possible to direct teaching to areas in which students need more help, rather than attempting to 'cover the content'.

Different CATs take different amounts of time during a lecture, from a few minutes at the beginning and end of a class session for the one-minute paper to 15 or 20 minutes for a complex CAT like the memory matrix. Some CATs, such as process self-analysis, are more effective if they are used outside of the class and discussed at the following class. The most important thing about using these strategies is that they are integrated into the learning process rather than being 'add-on' activities.

- *Why use these strategies at all? Is this 'hand-holding' necessary in higher education?* CATs provide opportunities to check on student learning before a critical stage: before the final exam, before a major project, or before a transition to a new subject upon which knowledge of a prior topic is crucial. Some lecturers might consider this 'hand-holding'. However, as Jarvis points out, 'Involving the student in judging what he or she has learnt encourages a more positive attitude to learning and increases the degree of student direction of the learning process' (Jarvis et al., 1998: 144). In other words, these strategies for checking on student learning are in some ways more rigorous for students because they put greater responsibility on them for monitoring and constructing their learning.

- *How do lecturers convince students that checking on their learning is worthwhile?* Lecturers have found that in the beginning students may be sceptical or may not take these strategies seriously because they are not graded. For this reason, it is important to explain what you are doing and why you are doing it: students' responses to CATs will allow you to help them to learn. If you find that a significant number of students clearly did not under-stand a key concept, the fact that you then spend more time on it, or approach it in a different way, will convince students that CATs are important and will help them to do well in graded assessments.

  Students also appreciate having opportunities to provide anonymous feedback to lecturers about what they are learning and what is confusing. Often students are hesitant to ask questions during a lecture. Studies on the use of CATs (Kelly, 1993; Cross and Steadman, 1996) indicate that students feel that the teacher 'really cares' about whether or not they are learning. This often makes them more motivated to learn. Students also believe that CATs make them more involved in learning because they are forced to think about what they have learned.

- *Is it necessary always to give feedback to students about their responses to CATs?* It is essential! Closing the feedback loop with students as quickly as possible is the most important part of the process. When students get feedback from lecturers, they know that lecturers are paying attention to their responses. As a lecturer reviews student feedback, usually at the begin-ning of the next lecture, students often find that others had similar questions. This can be comforting and can raise self-confidence among students who are having difficulties. Some lecturers base the entire next class on feedback to the students. This works particularly well for review/revision sessions. However, even taking five minutes at the beginning of a class is beneficial to the learning process. The most important thing is to ensure that students understand the lecturer's feedback, and that they know what to do with it (Sadler, 1989.)

- *How often should these strategies be used?* Some lecturers ask students to respond to a question at the end of every class, and others use CATs at critical points in the course or before a major exam or project. Most lecturers integrate the CATs as regular class activities. Others use them to evaluate the effectiveness of class activities or tests or to encourage students to evaluate their own learning progress. The frequency and type of CATs depends upon the students, the lecturer, the subject, the learning objectives and the reasons for asking students about their learning.

- *Do the students' responses have to be anonymous?* Anonymous feedback produces responses that are more candid. However, if the assessments take the form of homework assignments or small group activities within the class, anonymity is not possible and may not be necessary. Research on the use of these strategies indicates that students generally feel more comfortable if their responses are anonymous (Kelly, 1993).

- *What kind of questions should I ask?* It is best to ask students learner-centred questions ('What have you learned?') rather than teacher-centred questions ('How do you like my teaching?'). Responses to learner-centred questions show whether or not teaching is effective. Thoughtful, reflective questions are better than simple, factual ones. Questions should be asked only if you really want to know the answer and are willing to respond to feedback and to meet students' needs.

- *Is it necessary to have professional development before using these strategies?* Many lecturers started using CATs after reading the Cross and Angelo handbook (1993a) and selecting and adapting a few CATs for their lectures. However, CATs are even more effective for students if they are undertaken by a department or a course team. In this way, students have opportunities to respond to questions about their learning as they go through different lectures, seminars, tutorials and labs. Lecturers working together to integrate CATs into the curriculum find it very rewarding to share their experiences and work collaboratively as a group to improve teaching and learning.

Starting with a 'Teaching Goals Inventory' is a useful exercise for a group of lecturers who plan to implement CATs (Cross and Angelo, 1993b). This inventory helps to clarify teaching goals and learning objectives for individual lecturers or groups of lecturers working together in a departmental or course team. It can be an advantage to do some professional development as a group in order to learn about the various forms of CATs, and to decide which ones will be appropriate for enhancing learning in a specific course.

Conclusion

Using CATs has benefits for both students and lecturers. Students appreciate being asked what they are learning and what they do not understand. Using these strategies demonstrates to students that we care about their learning and want to facilitate their learning. However, lecturers using CATs also experience benefits. By asking students about their learning, lecturers can find out about their teaching and become more interested in the teaching and learning process in their discipline. This often leads to more discourse and enthusiasm about teaching and learning in departments and course teams, and this contributes to enhanced teaching and learning.

Websites on classroom assessment techniques

- American Association of Higher Education (AAHE) Assessment Forum: www.aahe.org/assessment/assesslinks.htm
- National Teaching & Learning Forum (NTLF): www.ntlf.com/html/lib/bib/assess.htm
- Technology applied to Classroom Assessments: www.ntlf.com/html/sf/vc75.htm
- Classroom Assessment Techniques designed for Technology: www.mtsu.edu/~itconf/Proceed99/Martin.htm

University websites on classroom assessment techniques

- Southern Illinois University: www.siue.edu/~deder/assess/catmain.html
- Hawaii Community College: www.hcc.hawaii.edu/intranet/committees/FacDevCom/guidebk/teachtip/assess-1.htm
  www.hcc.hawaii.edu/intranet/committees/FacDevCom/guidebk/teachtip/assess-2.htm
- Indiana University: www.iub.edu/~teaching/feedback.html – sfcats
- Iowa State University: www.cte.iastate.edu/tips/cat.html
- Pennsylvania State University: www.psu.edu/celt/CATs.html
- Portland State University: www.fd.pdx.edu/workshops/cat/examples.html
- Syracuse University: http://cstl.syr.edu/cstl/t-l/cls_asmt.htm
- University of New Orleans: http://ss.uno.edu/ss/TeachDevel/Asses/AssemTechMenu.html
- University of Washington: http://depts.washington.edu/cidrweb/CATools.htm

9

Reconsidering scholarship reconsidered

Glynis Cousin

In this chapter, I argue that Boyer's (1990) typology of scholarships (discovery, integration, application and teaching) contains problematic messages. On the one hand, this typology does much to raise the status of diverse forms of research activity, based as it is on Boyer's (1990: 24) plea for 'a more inclusive view of what it means to be a scholar'. On the other hand, it follows, implicitly, a hierarchical order that privileges the scholarship of discovery and thus a particular tradition of research. In spite of Boyer's insistence that all forms of scholarship should be valued and rewarded, a special place appears to be reserved for the 'scholarship of discovery'.

The scholarship of discovery Boyer (1990: 17) writes about is what is 'yet to be found ... the commitment to knowledge for its own sake, to freedom of inquiry and to following, in a disciplined fashion, an investigation wherever it may lead'. Arguably, this is a conventional view of curiosity driven, dispassionate, high status, funded research – closely aligned with a traditional view of the purpose of a university. Similar associations are made for the scholarship of integration, which is positioned as the scholarship of discovery's soulmate because its axis is 'original research': '... interpretation, fitting one's own research – or the research of others – into larger intellectual patterns ... serious, disciplined work that seeks to interpret, draw together, and bring new insight to bear on original research' (Boyer, 1990: 18,19).

These first two forms of scholarship appear to be ranked differently from Boyer's scholarships of application and teaching. To check my interpretations, I Internet surfed some definitions and found a wide range of interpretations, of which the following is a selection:

- A US faculty magazine, *Jaschick* (2005):
  Boyer ... argued that there were multiple forms of scholarship, *not just the form that produces new knowledge through laboratory break-throughs, journal articles or new books.* [my emphasis]
- An Australian faculty magazine (*CATL*, 1998):
  The scholarship of discovery is described as *what we most often think of as* scholarship, that is the pursuit of knowledge for its own sake, the

discovery of new knowledge ... at its most successful, [it] is seen by Boyer to play a major role in stimulating and engendering the intellectual climate of the institution. [my emphasis]

- A 'Pedablogue' (Arnzen, 2003):
  This element [discovery] of scholarship is purely investigative, in search of new information. At the core of scholarship, it is 'what contributes not only to the stock of human knowledge but also to the intellectual climate of a college or university' and Boyer considers investigation and research 'at the very heart of academic life' (Boyer, 1990, 17–18).

The scholarship of discovery in these interpretations is something that academics would all recognize, unthinkingly, much as plumbers would unthinkingly select from their toolbox a specific tool for a specific job. But it is the 'unthinking' bit that is increasingly problematic because it takes for granted a view that the Academy has some kind of consensus about what is meant by the scholarship of discovery. I will also argue that Boyer's scholarships of application and teaching are implicitly associated with a diminished view of qualitative research.

Discovery or construction?

The categories Boyer presents are not epistemologically neutral. In particular, the very idea that research can 'discover' has been in dispute for some time now; many researchers see the research process as making, rather than discovering, reality (Law, 2004; Denzin and Lincoln, 2007). In contrast, Boyer's conception of the scholarship of 'discovery' is deeply suggestive of an empiricist and objectivist framework. Within this framework, the researcher looks for a 'truth' that is judged to be knowable through the rigorous application of method; it constructs the ideal researcher as the one who is able to remove his or her subjectivity from the research in order to see dispassionately what is really happening 'out there' in the empirical world. Similarly, the ideal research site and subjects are selected and controlled for the elimination of what are thought to be contaminating factors. In short, research activity is treated as a technology that can discover laws in human society, which enable generalizations and predictions to be made. Such research is expected to involve strong quantitative and experimental dimensions. Randomized control trials are often held to be the gold standard within this tradition with, at best, a very peripheral place for qualitative research.

Contrasting views on discovery come from interpretivist and postmodernist researchers who argue that we cannot see and report on the empirical world objectively because we are part of it; our understandings are always mediated and negotiated. Such researchers accept that research always originates and is conducted in specific places, people and times, and that these affect their focus and interpretations. They are less drawn to the 'hard data romance' of empiricism (Wagner, 2007: 27), which involves the 'notion that, removed far enough from the social circumstances in which they were created, numbers and words are unambiguously objective'. Researcher investment in the research is never denied and is addressed by moves such as offering reflexive accounts of researcher positionality, an honest display of rival explanations, triangulation and an aspiration to generate under-standings rather than truths.

The critique of 'discovery research' represents a 'turn' in human enquiry, captured perhaps by the following pronouncement from Denzin and Lincoln (2007: 162): 'This is an age of emancipation; we have been freed from the confines of a single regime of truth and from the habit of seeing the world in one color.' The freedom is from the reign of empiricist and objectivist models of truth discovery towards the embracement of interpre-tivist and postmodern ones (Denzin and Lincoln, 2007); from notions of reliability and validity to those of reflexivity and trustworthiness; from the pursuit of confident generalization to that of fuzzy generalization (Bassey, 1999) or of 'petite generalization' (Stake, 1995); from 'method talk' to an acknowledgement that language makes us as much as we make it (Law, 2004); from rigour to mindful inquiry (Bentz and Shapiro, 1998); from deductive to inductive; from sites of controlled experimentation to natural-istic settings; and from evidence-based to evidence-informed.

Admittedly, these are crude oppositions which downplay the grey be-tween traditions. Some readers will also object to my lumping together intepretivist and postmodern approaches because there are disagreements about truth claims and researcher positionality across them. But reduced to a single and commonly held proposition, perhaps it could be summarized that human inquiry of any kind is understood by supporters of this turn to be a cultural practice that is inevitably, at some level, fictional. Morris (1999: 103, cited in Wagner, 2007: 33) expressed the mood well: 'Our choice, in so far as we have one, is not between fact and fiction, but between good and bad fiction'.

A central issue here is that of language. All research, whatever method it deploys, is a textual re-presentation of the reality it explores (Schostack, 2007). The scholarship of discovery is more likely to conceal this with a 'scientific realism' in which, argues Foley (1998: 110): '... the author must speak in the third person and be physically, psychologically, and ideologi-cally absent from the text. That lends the text an aura of omniscience. The all-knowing interpretive voice speaks from a distant, privileged vantage point in a detached, measured tone'.

Increasingly, the linguistic moves (notably the use of the passive and the third person) used within the discovery tradition are being rejected for a more foregrounded acknowledgement of the researcher's voice in the research process and the reporting. Incidentally, the results of this rejection are often judged against the standard of more conventional reports. In this way, genre becomes an indicator that surreptitiously demotes qualitative inquiry.

While you could locate interpretivist or postmodern forms of qualitative inquiry within Boyer's scholarship of discovery, it is a bit of a stretch. Such inquiry is more likely to be placed alongside Boyer's notions of the scholarship of application and of teaching. These scholarships are associated with client responsiveness, practice-based, local and reflective inquiry. While for Boyer, these research activities express distinctive forms of scholarship, for many, it is more a matter of a distinctive epistemology and purpose.

This confusion is explored by Shulman and Hutchins (1999: 13) who discuss an email they received from a Carnegie Scholar who questioned the wider credibility of his pedagogic research. It is worth quoting their response to this question this at length:

> One of the things we have learned from the work of the Carnegie Scholars is how hard it is for faculty, regardless of their own field and its rules of evidence, not to assume that credibility means a traditional social science model of inquiry. Part of the attractiveness of the social sciences comes from the fact that they cover a lot of methodological ground these days, having been extended and transformed over the years through the influence of fields such as anthropology, linguistics, and hermeneutics. They have been transformed, too, by the fact that most of the questions about human behavior we most want answered are not, in the end, 'science' questions, ones that lend themselves to immutable general truth, but rather questions about phenomena as they occur in local, particular contexts (like classrooms!). But to get at the fullest, deepest questions about teaching, faculty will have to learn and borrow from a wider array of fields and put a larger repertoire of methods behind the scholarship of teaching.

I see a tension in this statement. On the one hand, there is an acknowledgement that human inquiry has progressed in the ways described by Denzin and Lincoln (2007) and others; on the other hand, this acknowledgement is contrasted with 'science' questions that 'lend themselves to immutable general truth'. But the transformations in social science described by Lee and Shulman are also a challenge to the very idea that any questions can lend themselves to immutable general truth. Contrasting human inquiry with 'science' questions, risks preserving the primacy of the traditional model of the scholarship of discovery. In this quotation, scholars with reservations about the credibility of their work are reassured that there is a 'larger repertoire' on which to draw, but have they been reassured that doing so can produce work of equivalent value to that which has been traditionally assigned to the scholarship of discovery?

Mode 1 and 2 knowledge

Another dimension to this argument comes from those who argue that the nature of research activity has changed dramatically. In particular, the proponents of Mode I and 2 knowledge (Nowotny et al. 2000) argue that the former offers an outdated vision of a team of boffins working in the laboratory. Most research, these writers argue, does not conform to this image. Rather it is context sensitive, transdisciplinary, user responsive, C&IT exploitative, and it accepts that understandings generated by research will be provisional and will decay. In fact, Mode 2 knowledge looks something like Boyer's scholarship of application, but the growing claims are that Mode 2 is not secondary to discovery research, rather it is replacing it.

Theory driven and investigative practice-based?

There also appears to be a similar privileging of the scholarship of discovery by the UK-based Higher Education Academy (HEA), a national teaching and learning enhancement agency, which offers educational research funding to British universities. Bidders are required to select from two categories of research, namely 'practice and policy-based' or 'theory driven'. Here are extracts from the HEA (2008) calls for proposals:

> Theory-driven projects have the primary purpose of enhancing the conceptual or theoretical understanding which underpins the topic under investigation.

> The investigative practice-based and policy-based projects have the primary purpose of developing recommendations for action on issues, policies or practices within HE.

Bewilderingly, the HEA reassures the potential bidder that there may be practical application in theory driven projects and conceptual outcomes for practice- and policy-based ones. If this is so, it raises the question of why there should be a distinction? In particular, this division seems to overlook that academics' views of research as 'theory driven', 'investigative practice-based' or something entirely different depends largely on their epistemological stance. For instance, I would regard action research as 'theory driven' or at least 'theory generative', but there are others who would place it in the second HEA category (Cousin, 2000).

It seems to me that the HEA is asking bidders to commit themselves to specific pots and pans before they know what they want to cook. Theory in many qualitative approaches is seen as emergent rather than definitively embedded in the research design (e.g. Glaser and Strauss, [1967] 1999). More importantly, the quality of theory is not reliant on the kind of methodology or scale involved; rather, it is hooked into the quality of the research and of the researcher. Theory generation requires intellectual depth, researcher integrity and reflexivity, insight, persuasive and compelling argument, honest display of evidence, plausibility and acknowledgement of rival explanations. None of these are guaranteed by a specific research design any more than a pasta pot guarantees a good plate of pasta.

Perhaps the two HEA categories of research feed off Boyer's classifications in endorsing the view that 'real' research generates new knowledge (theory driven), while other forms of research (investigations) are worthy but not quite in the same league. The HES's opposition of 'research' and 'investigation' is both unhelpful and conceptually murky.

Particular and general

One of the unhappy outcomes of dividing the scholarship of discovery (or theory driven research) from other forms of scholarship is the damage it has done to the quality of local, naturalistic or practice-based research in higher education. I have often encountered the view that anyone can do this kind of research without giving much thought to theoretical engagement or to acquiring the necessary craft skills for its conduct. A particular casualty of this view is case study research, where often reports are no more than victory narratives of practice.

Misunderstandings about practice-based or applied research have produced a vicious circle, in which poor examples become the basis on which it is judged. The key misunderstanding among those who want to give local, single setting research the lowest status, centres on questions of generalization. Case study research is often thought to be of limited use in this respect; this betrays an ignorance about the purpose of this research as a 'science of the singular' (Simons, 1980), where the particular and general are treated as paradoxical rather than as counterposed. The paradox resides in the fact that it is precisely the case study researcher's attention to the depiction and analysis of the uniqueness of a case that allows a form of generalization to be made, not by the researcher but by the readers. Attention to the particular facilitates attention to the general: 'People can learn much that is general from single cases. They do that partly because they are familiar with other cases and they add this one in, thus making a slightly new group from which to generalize, a new opportunity to modify old generalizations' (Stake, 1995: 85).

A key aim of much qualitative research, then, is to offer a wealth of readable detail and analysis of a context, such that readers have the vicarious experience of being there; this experience allows readers to make what is called a 'naturalistic generalization'.

Another important facet of qualitative research is that it represents a search for meanings in contrast to quantitative or experimental methods. If qualitative research is understood to be primarily about scale (the single case, etc.), its purpose and capacity is misunderstood. Qualitative research is best seen as 'a systematic empirical inquiry into meaning' (Shank, 2002: 11) with decisions about scale being subordinated to this.

These subtle arguments about scale, meaning and generalization are often lost on those who are used to foregrounding numerical breadth and replication. Practically speaking, there needs to be more understanding about the scope and purpose of qualitative research and what it takes to produce good examples of it. This involves a recognition that qualitative research is not an accessory or subordinate to quantitative research but a field of inquiry with its own standards and aims. This does not appear to be fully understood by some academics who are encouraged, like the one writing to Shulman and Hutchings (1999) noted above, to engage in the scholarship of teaching.

It seems to me that we have created a licence in higher education research for qualitative research to be conducted in a 'spirit of careless rapture' (Coffey and Atkinson, 1996: 11), both with respect to theory and method. This is partly because we have associated it with forms of scholarship that are subordinated to a reified view of the scholarship of discovery. An exception might be some phenomenographic approaches that have strong deductive and procedural elements (Marton, 1981), which give it an air of science. The nub of my argument is that the epistemological positions lurking beneath Boyer's typology are ripe for disturbance. To repeat Shulman and Hutchings (1999: 13), we need to 'get at the fullest, deepest questions about teaching … from a larger repertoire of methods', and this involves generating a refreshed debate about the scholarship of teaching.

To conclude, Boyer's (1990) book *Scholarship Reconsidered* provided education, faculty developers, academics and institutions with important arguments to support the notion of a rounded academic. We owe a huge debt to Boyer for his promotion of research and scholarship into university teaching. To fully exploit the considerable fruits of this promotion, we must be apace with contemporary epistemological debates. There is a good chance that, were he alive today, Boyer would agree with this call, since his views were never entrenched and always thoughtful.

10

Doing small-scale qualitative research on educational innovation

Sarah Skerratt

Introduction

This chapter is designed for those who aim to generate qualitative evidence in relation to improvements and innovations in higher education and student learning. It is also for those who want to 'dip into' qualitative inquiry, using some of the tools either for a stand-alone small research project or as part of a larger investigation.

I have assumed that the reader of this chapter will know how to frame research questions or hypotheses, but is unsure about whether a qualitative approach 'fits' what they want to do, and, if it does, how to apply it to their project. I focus on how to make research design decisions, while highlighting how much you can (and cannot) say from this type of research in this area.

The chapter is structured around the main elements of planning, carrying out the research and writing up findings. I conclude by defining minimum requirements for sound, small-scale qualitative research on teaching and learning in higher education. In order to illustrate how these elements operate in practice, I will cite three examples of small-scale qualitative research published in the journal *Active Learning in Higher Education*:

- Jowett, A. (2005) Did the market force Subject Review? A case study, *Active Learning in Higher Education*, 6(1): 73–86
- East, R. (2005) A progress report on progress files: the experience of one higher education institution, *Active Learning in Higher Education*, 6(2): 160–71
- Castles, J. (2004) Persistence and the adult learner: factors affecting persistence in Open University students, *Active Learning in Higher Education*, 5(2): 166–79.

These examples were selected in order to illustrate both the types of research projects that academics can carry out as part of their teaching commitments (East, 2005), and projects that are deliberately designed, funded and carried out (Castles, 2004; Jowett, 2005). I point to strengths in these authors' qualitative inquiries, and suggest ways in which their reporting could be strengthened.

Planning your research focus

As for any piece of research, it is crucial to think through why you want to do a particular project on teaching and learning in higher education. Why do you think it is necessary? What do you feel your contribution is likely to be? What are your key questions? Answering these questions begins to focus and structure your research framework and set boundaries.

The first step is to describe your aim – in one sentence. Second, outline two to three research hypotheses or questions, identifying why they are important: for example, because of something you read in wider research literature; because it is important to test a particular practice and report these findings to your peers and/or to a wider (policy/practice) audience. This locates your work in a context of research on teaching and learning in higher education, as illustrated in the three examples that follow:

1 Jowett (2005) describes the 'bigger picture', explaining how there has been extensive discussion around 'expansion versus quality' in the higher education (HE) sector. He highlights the Jarrett Report (1985), which linked future development of HE with the introduction of performance indicators (PIs), which in turn could inform consumers' choices. He then defines the focus of his study: 'this study seeks to explore the views of a cohort of academic staff regarding the external Quality Assurance process of Subject Review [SR]'. He then defines the boundaries of his research: 'this paper provides a detailed insight of how a particular staff cohort believes that SR might influence HE practice and quality and affect the position of their Department in the market'. We now have a clear idea of this study's topic and sample.

2 East's (2005) introduction states: 'The UK higher education sector is currently committed to each higher education institution (HEI) implementing a system of progress files for students on all taught courses' (p.160), where progress files are 'a central feature of Personal Development Planning (PDP)' (p.161). As well as citing the 'official' literature, East also highlights where concerns have been raised. He then delimits the discussion to an examination of the implementation of progress files, and then to the experience of one institution. Again, we now have a clear indication of topic and sample for the study.

3 Castles (2004) outlines 'attrition rates' in adult learning, particularly in distance and open learning, pointing to two research threads: (i) student drop-out and (ii) persistence (p.166). She then tells us that her focus is a

qualitative study testing factors identified in the literature as contributing to persistence. She states her more detailed point of focus: 'this research is as much concerned with the identification of factors leading to success as it is with discovering reasons for withdrawal' (p.167). And then further: 'If the factors contributing to the profile of a successful student could be identified, prioritised or weighted, better course or career advice could be given to intending and continuing students ... identifying the optimum conditions for adult study. This research attempts to identify these factors, how they interact with each other and how students might prioritize them' (p.167).

For more detail on defining a research focus for qualitative studies, see Denscombe (2001).

Planning your research approach

Having set the framework, you can then identify how you will generate data to address your aim and hypotheses or research questions. First, consider whether to use a quantitative or qualitative approach, or a combination of the two (see chapters 11 and 12). If you want to find answers to 'how many', 'what' and 'when' type of questions, such as commenting on trends across a large (50-plus) set of staff or students, then quantitative methods are appropriate. By contrast, a qualitative approach allows you to find answers to 'why' questions. For example, if you want to comment in-depth on staff or student responses to a particular practice, you will want to capture the words they use/do not use, and the reasons behind them. Castles (2004) outlines her approach:

> Based on the literature review ... to try to separate the most important factors from those that might be less useful for consideration, and also to test some of the anomalies in the literature, it was decided to gather qualitative information through interviews with a sample of OU students. (p.173)

It is interesting to note Castle's (2004) use of the term 'to test'; in qualitative research, typically, we would use the terms 'to understand', 'to explore' or 'to explain'.

The qualitative research toolkit – gathering your data

Qualitative research offers an extensive 'toolkit'. See, for example, Patton (2001); Creswell (2002 and 2007); Ritchie and Lewis (2003); and Denzin and Lincoln (2007). Small-scale research projects are carried out within fairly tight resource (time and money) constraints, so the 'purest' form of these tools, such as ethnography and grounded theory (Glaser and Strauss, [1967] 1999; Creswell, 2007) is unlikely to be feasible.

You need to document your choice of tools, since in the qualitative tradition data are not seen as 'existing'; instead, qualitative researchers construct data through their investigations. We do this through the questions we ask, the way we ask them and the data we judge to be 'relevant' or 'irrelevant'. All of this is based on the qualitative researcher's implicit judgements, and these must therefore be clarified, as must the basis for those judgements. The following quotes illustrate two approaches:

> The schedule was partially prescribed by pre-existing data, that is, a 'tighter design' … However, there was enough flexibility in the questionnaire to allow respondents to talk about the areas they perceived to be connected to their responses or to provide any extra information. It was thus hoped that the inductive approach would not be entirely abandoned. (Castles, 2004: 173)

> East (2005) outlines steps he took as part of his job: the audit in the institutions, the identification and emergence of 'champions', the establishment of a Progress Files Steering Group to advise on implementation, a review of the literature on Progress Files, visits to other HEIs, attendance at PDP conferences, and early attempts to use progress files with students: 'All these were steps to Progress Files becoming university policy in spring 2003'. There was to be a subsequent rolling out of progress files across the University in 2005–2006, so 14 pilots studies were established in 2002–2003. (East, 2005).

Castles (2004) has outlined implications of methodological decisions for her research, and East (2005) demonstrates a more pragmatic approach, based on work objectives.

Process of inquiry

Small-scale qualitative inquiry usually (but not always) follows the process of inquiry shown in Figure 10.1.

In describing this process, I will assume the reader is familiar with how to carry out a desk study or literature review (Hart, 1998 and 2001). I will therefore focus in this section on data collection, management and presentation.

Primary data collection

Observation, individual and group interviews can be combined to generate complementary data types. They may also be used as parts of a process, for example, by starting with group interviews, followed by in-depth one-to-one interviews.

Process of inquiry →

1   Desk study (or secondary data collection)

2   Primary data collection:

    a   (Participant) observation

    b   Semi-structured interviews (individuals)

    c   Group interviews (focus groups)

3   Data management:

    a   Coding

    b   Analysis

4   Presentation of findings

5   Discussion of findings and their implications

Figure 10.1 Process of inquiry for a small-scale qualitative inquiry

(Participant) observation is a form of observation where researchers deliberately participate in and observe the activities they are researching. This gives them first-hand experience and also allows them to ask questions and increase their understanding of processes. It generates data about how and why people are/not interacting in certain settings, how body language is/not expressed, how certain issues are/not talked about, and why certain people are involved in (or excluded from) certain processes. Different types of observations can be made:

- Re-observe the same situation with different people
- Re-observe the same people in a different situation
- Observe situations or people repeatedly over time (longitudinal analysis).

Individual interviews

Typically, a semi-structured approach is used. The research aim and hypotheses are reformulated into a list of four to five themes that then become the interviewer's prompt sheet, with sub-points for follow up questions, as appropriate. Ensuring these links between aims, themes and prompts allows researchers to make connections between what people say in interviews and the research focus.

Interviews last between one and two hours, during which you steer interviewees through the themes, creating space for them to respond in their own way. Interviewees will also talk about issues important to them, which may appear to be 'deviations'. However, underlying this approach is the recognition that, although you have some idea of the range of issues, you do not know them all, and you are thus reliant on interviewees enlightening you about the complexities and reasons behind their thoughts and behaviours. Qualitative inquiry is structured around a desire to identify the 'unexpected' and the 'taken-for-granted assumptions that are part one's culture' (Cohen, 1994). Jowett (2005) and Castles (2004) are examples of this approach:

> Jowett aimed to: 'discover both the form and reasons for staff percep-
> tions'; he selects a semi-structured interview format: 'the interviews
> were conducted as an open discussion of the issues of SR and how they
> impinge on the Department ... An interview guide based on the aims
> of the study and the issues in the SR handbook was referred to during
> the interviews to centre the discussion on key topics. Nonetheless, the
> respondents' ideas were the focus so the path of each interview was
> unique' (Jowett, 2005: 75).
>
> Castles states that the semi-structured interview was 'flexible enough
> to allow respondents to enlarge upon areas of their lives that they felt
> to be important' (Castles, 2004: 173).

There is a range of prompt types, from asking about current situations, reflections on past occurrences, and hypothetical questions of 'What would you do if ...?' Further, interviews typically take place in the 'home environment' of the interviewee, rather than in a 'laboratory' situation:

> Castles helpfully explains the challenges of using different recall
> processes and hypothetical scenarios, in terms of data reliability
> (p.174). In addition, 'Students were interviewed in their homes at a
> time of their choosing and all agreed that the interviews should be
> recorded' (Castles, 2004: 175).

Recording and note-taking are options for ensuring that maximum data are acquired. It is essential to ask permission before recording, observe the extent to which the interviewee is hindered, and to stop recording if the interviewee feels uncomfortable. It is advisable to take notes as back-up.

Group interviews

If you are interested in how people discuss an issue with one another, such as peer assessment, and you want to see whether people talk about it in a certain way, if certain people are more vocal than others, or express different concerns than others, then the group setting is ideal.

Typically, group interviews run for up to two hours. As facilitator, you steer participants, within the agreed time-frame, through your prepared themes and allow for discussion of (to you) unexpected issues. You ensure that all participants are given equal opportunity to contribute. A shared complicity can develop in groups, whereby the most articulate or forceful person dominates and others try but then cease to contribute. You need to generate and manage a friendly, inclusive environment, interrupting when necessary, even asking some people to stop talking and others to contribute. It can be useful to establish these 'ground rules' at the beginning, before the start of the discussion.

If resources permit, it can be useful to have an assistant take notes, since your focus is on managing group dynamics. An additional colleague can ensure observations or data are not missed. If you decide to make a recording, ensure that your equipment is satisfactory for 10–12 people's voices, and ask everyone to introduce themselves (first names only) to give a name for each voice. It is best to test recording equipment beforehand, and to take notes on a flipchart or note pad.

Sampling: who do you interview?

There are three main approaches to sampling in qualitative research: purposive, illustrative and snowball sampling.

1 *Purposive sampling* is sampling with a purpose. 'Purpose' in this context has a subtly different meaning from bias: you select specific people because they have reflected on a practice or method and are likely to have an opinion.
2 *Illustrative sampling* is used when you want to illustrate the views of different groups of people (staff, young undergraduates, part-time learners, mature students, distance learners, etc.). You select a similar number in each of these categories (you may want a 'quota' of each), and your findings illustrate responses from these different groups.
3 *Snowball sampling* is a process of moving from your initial sample towards the selection of individuals and groups who are suggested to you by interviewees. Again, steps are taken to ensure that such snowballing does not lead to bias by following through on those who would give only one viewpoint. The snowballing approach is still 'traceable', and the researcher can account for why certain individuals were/were not selected for interview.

Qualitative sampling is not designed to be statistically representative; you are not aiming to say that the people you interviewed (such as a group of peer lecturers) are representative of that type (i.e. of all lecturers at your university or college). Therefore, it is important to explain your sample, its rationale and any implications of your sampling frame by telling the reader:

- Who you interviewed and why
- Who you chose not to interview
- How many people you interviewed and from which organizations, groups or locations.

Usually, this can go in an appendix as a list of interviewee types. Information about sampling allows the reader to be confident that you have not biased your research by only interviewing those who are likely to agree with a proposed teaching and learning method, and demonstrates that you have ensured that a range of views is accessed, as illustrated by Jowett (2005):

Jowett interviewed 15 out of 21 academic staff and later notes that 'Twenty-two hours of interview yielded a considerable quantity of data'. He describes the range of staff types he interviewed, and includes a brief description of non-participant types in the department (Jowett, 2005: 75).

Castles (2004) outlines her sampling frame; she is interested in geographical location, gender and extent of completion:

Castles specified where geographically the sampled students were from; however, she did not state why the particular region was selected, and what the implications were, if any, of its selection (e.g. typical, atypical) (p.173). She described her sample as comprising: '12 students, 6 male and 6 female. The group was sub-divided into those who had completed, those who had formally withdrawn and those who had left without notifying the university' (Castles, 2004: 174–5).

When selecting people for group interviews, use the same sampling approaches. In addition, you are responsible for assembling groups that are likely to flow well; it is best not put people together who are likely to argue or be uncomfortable in each other's presence, or where hierarchical positions make it difficult for senior or junior staff to be open.

Sampling: how many do you interview?

There is no 'right number' of interviewees. Twenty is considered a fairly large sample for qualitative work, because each interview generates several pages of data. For group interviews eight people per group is ideal, with 12 being the maximum.

Budget may determine the number of individual and group interviews. Some researchers pay group participants a fee for taking part, pay their travel expenses and/or serve food or other light refreshments. Sometimes there can be a fee for hiring a venue for interviews. There are also potential costs in administration, setting up, transcription and analysis of data. However, less than four to six individual interviews may start to jeopardize the validity of your data. Further, you may find that after a certain number of interviews, no new findings appear because you have saturated the range of issues; some researchers use 'saturation sampling' to determine the cut-off point.

Another sampling decision is whether to run group interviews with already established groups or with groups that have been set up for your research. The pros with the former are that trust and ease of communication are usually well established; however, subtle hierarchies can exist that inhibit free-flowing discussion. Conversely, with new groups hierarchies are less likely to form during the session, but you have to contend with initial awkwardness. Your choice depends on whether an already established group represents an advantage to your research.

Transcription, coding of data and thematic analysis

Once the observation and/or interview stage is completed, you will have generated a wealth of rich textual material. If you have linked the themes of your interviews to your original aim and hypotheses, your data will automatically be divisible into those themes. Observational data is harder to incorporate into themes, but it is still possible to do so by reading and rereading your notes.

First, it is best to type your notes from observation, and your notes or transcripts from individual and group interviews, and to read them several times so that you are extremely familiar with your data. Second, using the original research questions or hypotheses as 'themes', assign theme codes or labels to your data: where a sentence or paragraph fits into a theme, label it with a short-hand tag; pieces of data can have more than one tag. It is important to 'allow' codes, themes, topics or keywords to emerge from the data ('emic codes'), as well as using the already decided codes ('etic codes') to categorize your data. Combining emic and etic is ideal, and this is why it is essential to be extremely familiar with the data. Third, group all responses under Theme 1, all responses under Theme 2, and so on. Fourth, focus on each theme separately: within Theme 1, code/tag data into emerging sub-groups. You are not looking only for agreement within your data, but also for 'negative cases', in other words, responses that do not conform with the dominant respondent view. Jowett (2005) and Castles (2004) illustrate these processes in teaching and learning research:

'... with the consent of respondents, all interviews were tape recorded and detailed written notes were taken' (Jowett: 75); interview tapes were transcribed within a week. Jowett's coding process was as follows: 'Notes and transcripts were read line by line and ... each new theme became a category and each related phrase was fragmented and indexed into a cell of a word processor table. All of the interview data were collated into this table finally containing 1181 phrases sieved into 134 preliminary categories. The categories within the table were reviewed and compared with one another and those with similar themes coalesced. The exercise was repeated twice, reducing the data to 36 categories' (p. 75). Jowett then adds: 'Relevant data were collated into seven categories core to the study and the remainder, where discussion had strayed beyond the study, discarded' (p. 75). Jowett's use of the terms 'relevant' and 'the remainder' was potentially premature at this stage in the report (Jowett, 2005).

Castles outlines her data coding processes, showing rigour and thus increasing the reader's confidence in the reliability of the data. She talks of minimizing bias that might have been caused by the researcher's approach to the analysis (p. 175). She describes 'descriptive coding', based on factors from the literature, plus inductive comments made by researcher, and 'inferential coding', numbers indicating the level of importance attached to this issue by the interviewee (Castles, 2004).

When you type up your notes, it is important to assign a unique code to each interviewee. This can reflect the type of interviewee, for example, ST01 (Student 01), LE01 (Lecturer 01). When you cut and paste pieces of data into one or more themes and sub-themes, type the interviewee code with that piece of data. These codes give extra flavour and perspective when you cite quotes in your reporting.

Using computer databases

There is no rule about use or non-use of computer-based qualitative databases for organizing and retrieving data. If you are planning to carry out repeated qualitative projects, it would be worth investing your time in learning a new programme such as nVivo, Ethnograph or Atlas-ti.

- nVivo software link: www.qsrinternational.com/support_downloads.aspx
- Ethnograph software link: www.qualisresearch.com/
- Atlas-ti software link: www.atlasti.com/

However, if yours is a single project of say 15 interviews, then it is fairly straightforward to use a word processing package, copying and pasting from individual interview files into the analysis structure. Copying and pasting – rather than cutting and pasting – ensures that the original transcripts/notes intact. This means that you will be able to refer back to the context in which something was said. The processes of assigning codes and grouping data are manual tasks that you must carry out whether you use computer databases or word processing. Some databases are designed to combine text, sounds and images, which can be similarly labelled. If you are presenting visual stimuli (such as photographs of a teaching style), and want to link response data to the stimuli, these databases can help.

Reporting your findings

The coding and analysis described above is called 'thematic analysis' (Patton, 1986 and 2001), because you identify themes in your data and organize your data within them. Similarly, in reporting findings, it is best to present them thematically.

In qualitative research, we do not have statistical tools for showing 'significance' of findings; the researcher indicates these attributes. Some authors begin with themes around which there is resounding consensus, or those themes which, whilst mentioned by all interviewees, contain contrasting views. These are seen as 'primary' themes; authors then report secondary and tertiary themes:

> First level of importance: identify the factor which was mentioned by all interviewees, either positively or negatively. Second level of importance: a range of factors, including a new factor which emerged (love of learning). At the third level of importance, 6 factors identified ...
> (Castles, 2004: 176)

Another approach is to use your research questions or hypotheses as theme headings. Your choice will depend on how you want to tell the story – do the research questions or hypotheses progress well from one issue to the next, or do the emerging themes capture the issues better? In both cases, you will show:

- Themes mentioned by the majority
- Areas of consensus within themes and sub-themes
- The range and diversity of responses.

Analysis and reporting thus show the 'messiness' of issues, the 'noise' in the system; it is not designed for neat tying-up of all loose ends. Castles (2004), in the preceding quote, mentioned the positive and negative cases, and that a new factor had emerged. Jowett (2005) also states that:

Qualitative analysis of these data revealed a spectrum of attitudes to Subject Review ... There is agreement on drivers of process but not on whether this process was desirable ... This sample of staff ... are generally supportive of the principle of SR although dubious about the precise methods. (Jowett, 2005: 81)

Using quotations

It is usual to illustrate themes and sub-themes with verbatim quotes from interviews. These are not intended to imply a uniform voice; rather, they expand points you are communicating. When citing a verbatim quote, use the interviewee code at the end of the quotation (such as LT01 or ST01); some researchers also put age, education level, gender or another descriptor derived from the analysis (e.g. from a typology of participants such as 'completer, withdrawer or leaver'), since it gives helpful, contextual signposting for the reader.

Maintaining confidentiality

It is crucial to ensure that readers cannot identify individuals. Interviewee codes need to reflect interviewee types rather than identifiable roles; any locational information or names in a quote which would indicate an individual should be removed, unless participants consent to being identified through signed consent forms. This is particularly important for sensitive issues, for small communities (such as rural settings) or small professional groups (a department of colleagues or specific cohort of students).

Limitations

It can be tempting to say more from your data than is appropriate. For example, if you have interviewed a cohort of 14 students aged 19–20 on an archaeology course at a specific department in one university at a particular point in time, your findings can only relate to those individuals in that given context. It is not possible, based on these data, to apply your conclusions to all students aged 19–20 on archaeology courses. Instead, you can propose that further research is required to ascertain whether this extrapolation is accurate. The following quotes are contrasting: Jowett (2005) limits what he can say, while East (2005) implicitly extrapolates from his study of one University to the wider HE sector:

It is impossible to assume that this case study reflects the views of staff in all departments and HE institutions ... (Jowett, 2005: 84)

Negative attitudes are likely to increase if staff involvement in this process is seen as imposing an additional burden on busy academics who, in the last decade or so, have had to deal, inter alia, with the additional responsibilities attendant on the move to a system of mass higher education. (East, 2005)

There is also a need to distinguish between findings and opinions, otherwise the reader is distracted by trying to assess the authenticity of the findings, while also taking in the findings themselves. The following examples unfortunately do not make this distinction, meaning that it is impossible to know the basis of these statements:

> 'While [the pilot approach] increased the amount of staff time absorbed by the tutor system ... no additional resources were made available for this. On most of the pilot studies therefore, use was made of "champions", those lecturers who saw the benefits of PDP and the use of progress files and were thus prepared to go the "extra mile".
>
> 'Providing staff who engage in PDP and progress files with some formal recognition ... might not only enhance their self worth but also send a message to other staff about the value being placed on this' (East, 2005: 167–8).

This lack of clarity weakens the arguments put forward and is not an advisable style of reporting. Emotive phrasing is also inadvisable, since it makes the reader more reluctant to accept the findings:

> East (2005) states an emotive conclusion about the potential for 'sham development' of 'symbolic' PDPs ... and re-emphasizes the 'additional responsibility without resources issue', again, without citing evidence.

In contrast, analysis is strengthened by comparing findings with others from the literature and suggesting how the research could be extended:

> 'staff explained how the department benefited from its location and this probably strengthened its position in the market and enabled it to attract an excess of UCAS applicants. This confirms

the view of Tight (2000) that in certain institutions geographical factors are more important than high SR scores' (Jowett, 2005: 81–2).

'the findings are largely in accordance with those of other studies'.

'General theories on the impact of SR, or other QA processes, may be drawn if the study were extended by "triangulation". This requires further sampling to enrich the data' (Jowett, 2005: 84–5).

Concluding comments

Using examples from higher education teaching and learning research, I have outlined three main elements of carrying out small-scale qualitative research. In conclusion, minimum requirements for sound small-scale qualitative research include:

1 Plan your research, identify your focus and delimit its boundaries
2 Decide if you are asking 'why?' or 'what/how many'?
3 Document your research process, including why you have chosen certain tools
4 Ensure your sampling is unbiased
5 Use thematic analysis to code and report your data and findings
6 Show diversity of responses, including negative cases, and use direct quotes
7 Do not extrapolate without foundation, and differentiate opinions from findings.

11

Doing small-scale quantitative research on educational innovation

Ruth Lowry

Introduction

The aim of this chapter is not to provide a 'how to' guide to performing statistical procedures, but rather to discuss how quantitative research methodology can be used to structure the evidence gathered in your role as an evidenced-based educator. This will assume that you are currently employing quantitative methodology in your research and have an understanding of the area. Therefore, I will not discuss the intricacies of or critique certain types of methods or analysis, but rather I will show how they can be employed to gather evidence for your teaching practice. I will consider the research process and key decisions to be made when planning educational quantitative research. I will then examine these in practice, using examples of papers on teaching and learning in higher education, published in a range of disciplines.

The three examples selected from a number of higher education journals explore the evaluation of different uses of technology in teaching and learning in higher education:

- Azzawi, M. and Dawson, M.M. (2007) The effectiveness of lecture-integrated, web-supported case studies in large group teaching, *Bioscience Education eJournal, 10*
- Choi, H.J. and Johnson, S.D. (2006) The effect of problem-based video instruction on learner satisfaction, comprehension and retention in college students, *British Journal of Educational Technology*, 38: 885–95
- Morling, B., McAuliffe, M., Cohen, L. and DiLorenzo, T.M. (2008) Efficacy of personal response systems ('Clickers') in large introductory psychology classes, *Teaching of Psychology*, 35: 45–50.

Quantitative methods are common in scientific, empirical investigations and use numeric data. Therefore, the methods for collecting and analysing information are descriptive (summarizing or reducing the information collected to indicate patterns and trends) and inferential (making inferences from the data collected to wider populations) statistics. These principles can also be applied to your role as an educator, in terms of how you gather evidence of the impact of your work on students' learning. This may involve a shift from science, for example, to social science. In social science the absolutes of measurement and experimentation are contextualized. In this area, 'research' consists of observing and monitoring, rather than controlling the variables of interest.

Research planning

1 Ethical considerations: what needs to be addressed before you start?
2 The research question: identifying your objective
3 Measurement: transforming concepts into tangible variables
4 Research design: applying control to the research process
5 Analysis: methods for interpreting data.

Ethical considerations: what needs to be addressed before you start?

A key factor in any research planning is the process of ethical approval and funding. Whilst this chapter is not the place to consider ethics and funding in detail, it is worth noting that detailed planning of the methods, data collection and analysis are required as part of any ethics or funding submission, when human participants are involved. This is generally taken to include research projects on teaching and learning in higher education.

When planning your study, consider what information is naturally available to you in your capacity as an academic and therefore does not require the informed consent of participants (take the Azzawi and Dawson, 2007, and the Morling et al., 2008, papers as examples). When comparing teaching methods, you will need to satisfy ethical reviewers that certain students are not disadvantaged by being assigned to particular treatment or condition groups. Therefore, you may need to consider whether additional support should be offered to some participants after data collection is completed.

Many ethical scrutiny panels and grant awarding bodies require a power calculation of required sample size for quantitative investigations. Be clear about how you calculated sample size, as social science studies can vary significantly from those of the pure sciences. An examination of previous, related studies and reference to social science and educational research methods textbooks will assist in the process, and shareware programmes downloaded from the Internet can calculate sample size for you (e.g. GPower).

The research question: identifying your objective

At the risk of stating the obvious, the first stage of any research project is the grand idea that will translate into the research objective or question. This universal truth should be employed with your scholarly enquiries as much as your research activities. Think about the main issue you want to study, and keep this to the fore; this is particularly important when time is scarce and you need to think strategically about your work. Having a firm concept of the parameters of your study allows you to remain focused on the key measures and outcomes, rather than getting lost in a myriad possible causes or relationships. In this way you will gain competence and confidence in your scholarship in this area, before snowballing activities in future large-scale research.

From the research question you can begin your literature search to find out what is known in the area about your concept, and this leads to the development of a plan of enquiry. Again, by having a clear focus, you are less likely to fall into the trap of tangential enquiry and losing sight of the key issues to be examined. Reading related papers in the higher education literature will develop your knowledge of what research designs, measures and analyses are employed in the area.

If we examine the research questions used in the three examples we find a range of levels of detail:

Azzawi and Dawson (2007)

'The effectiveness of lecture-integrated and web-supported case studies in supporting a large and academically diverse group of undergraduate students' (abstract, line 1). This makes it clear that the study will explore two methods of delivering case studies and examine how effective these methods were with different groups of students.

Choi and Johnson (2006)

'identify the effects of two major components (i.e. video and group discussion) of problem-based video instruction on college students' learning' (p. 885). This articulates the researcher's interest in students' learning through two modes of problem-based video instruction (PBVI), which would be suited to an experimental or quasi-experimental design.

Morling et al. (2008)

'Personal hand-held responders, commonly called "clickers" are one of the latest rends in technology for teaching' (p. 45). As the paper develops it becomes clear what is under investigation. However, there is a lack of clarity at the beginning of the paper as to which aspect of efficacy is to be explored with regard to clickers. This weakens the rationale for the study.

Measurement: transforming concepts into tangible variables

As in other areas, for quantitative research on teaching and learning the concepts that are to be measured must be precisely defined (operationalized), be they objective physical measures (such as attendance – number of sessions attended over a semester – or assessment grades – classification or percentage) or subjective measures (such as satisfaction or self-esteem – psychometric measures with acceptable reliability and validity). Once you have these operational definitions for your measures, it is possible to set out the formal, specific and concise research or experimental hypotheses to be tested. By using similar methods to other researchers you will not only be able to comment on your own study's findings but also be able to draw conclusions about similarities or discrepancies between your work and others'.

The first variable to consider is the dependent variable. Which aspect of teaching and learning do you want to measure, predict or evaluate? In educational research a number of key outcome variables recur in the literature that practitioners routinely think about improving, reducing, modifying or changing through their work:

- Student performance in assessment
- Student attendance, retention and attrition
- Student satisfaction and evaluation of experiences
- Key skills, e.g. engagement with technology, literacy and numeric activities
- Psychological skills, e.g. concentration, attention, motivation or behaviour.

Academics who are module leaders or course directors generally collect some or all of these variables as a matter of course. Other variables may require additional data collection, but you can search the literature and ask colleagues for examples of validated, standardized measures.

As in a lab-based experiment, it is essential to consider the nature and quality of the variables to be examined. The qualities or properties of variables will determine the sophistication of the analyses that can be performed and ultimately the type of conclusions that you can draw. Discrete (nominal or ordinal) variables will limit the forms of analysis to non-parametric methods, whereas continuous (interval or ratio) variables will allow for parametric analysis. Therefore, consideration should be given to what you are going to ask: can the information be collected in a continuous form and later transformed into discrete categories if that is more appropriate? It will always be possible to reduce data, but it is not possible to elaborate on data, post-collection. Try not to go past the point of no return in your research, where you are then forced to analyse data in such a way that makes it difficult to draw firm assertions. The three illustrative papers examined the following variables:

Azzawi and Dawson (2007)

1 The dependent variable was student learning support
   • Perceived usefulness measured using evaluation questionnaire (5-point Likert scale)
   • Student access of Web-supported material (intranet page hits)
   • Student performance in summative assessment

2 The independent variable was the undergraduate course of study, namely one of three BSc courses and one HND course in the biological sciences.

The authors clearly set out what they were examining and how the variables were measured. The data collected made use of the information readily available to the module coordinators and therefore did not add greatly to what was already in place.

Choi and Johnson (2006)

1 The dependent variable was students' learning
   • Learner satisfaction, which was a total score from seven self-report items (drawn from the Instructional Materials Motivation Survey by Keller, 1987)
   • Comprehension and retention were measured by assessment of the class tasks (total score on tests)

2 The independent variable was PBVI – participants were randomly assigned to one of three groups or levels of PBVI. All received a lecture that was subsequently reinforced by the three methods: group 1 received the PBVI and a group discussion, group 2 received the PBVI without group discussion, and group 3 received a problem-based text message instruction.

Very clear and precise definitions are given regarding the variables under investigation and how they were measured, with fuller detail provided in the methodology. The use of three groups provided a control and minimal intervention with which to compare the treatment condition, strengthening the study and conclusions.

Morling et al. (2008)

- The primary dependent variable was exam score, as measured by two exam scores
- Supplementary dependent variables were interest and engagement, as measured by self-report course evaluation
- The independent variable was the use of a clicker or traditional answering of multiple choice questions.

As in the Azzawi and Dawson (2007) article, the definitions used are straightforward, and the research makes use of readily available data, collected in the course of teaching

Research design: applying control to the research process

While there are few opportunities for truly experimental research in the form of randomized controlled trials in scholarly research, there are opportunities to employ a range of other research designs. Typically, observational or correlational studies are reported where the researcher has made use of naturally occurring information and draws inferences based on relationships between the variables measured. Other examples are cross-sectional and quasi-experimental designs, where randomization cannot be employed in allocating students to conditions. When designing your research project and deciding on the interaction between the dependent variable and independent variable, consider how the independent variable can be manipulated or controlled to measure the dependent variable. The following Table 11.1 provides examples of how traditional scientific method designs can be contextualized in studies of teaching and learning in higher education.

As stated at the beginning of the chapter, initial, focused planning about your research objective will create a tightly framed and manageable project. This need not be too complex a design, as that can lead to complications in the analysis stage, when constraints such as power and sample size play a pivotal role in the conclusions that can be drawn.

Table 11.1   Examples of research design in educational research

Design	Example
Correlational	Relationship between parental income and graduate debt.
Cross-sectional	Differences in part-time employment of students who live at home and those who rent.
Quasi-experimental	Differences between online and face to face tutorial support for student learning. It is not feasible to randomly assign students from the same cohort to different conditions, so different cohorts are used.
Experimental	Influence of tutor experience on student performance. Students are randomly assigned to one of three tutor groups at the start of the semester.
Independent (between groups)	Comparison of feedback on performance. Provide one group with corrective and one group with summative feedback on an assignment. Then measure performance in a second task.
Repeated (within groups)	Differences in the number of hours of revision students do for three modules. Only involves one group of students, following them through the different stages.
Factorial	Interaction between gender and maturity of students in terms of readiness to study. Gender has two levels (male, female). Maturity has three levels (school leavers, gap students and mature students). Reported as a 2 x 3 between-groups factorial design.

In the cases of the three examples, the research design was as follows:

Azzawi and Dawson (2007)

- *Cross-sectional design*: The study observed naturally occurring variables, such as degree type and A-level qualifications, and then examined the difference between these groups of students on the key dependent variable. This involved no experimental manipulation.

- *Total sample size was 264*: Although this was a good sample size for examining students accessing Web-based material and summative assessment, the results show that only 75 students completed the evaluation. This small proportion of the total cohort limits the extent to which the authors can generalize from their study.

Choi and Johnson (2006)

- *Between-group post-test-only experimental design*: In the methodology section the researchers clearly set out the experimental design and participant allocation to the various groups. Their use of a post-test-only design makes it difficult to know if the randomization of participant group selection produced a balance of participants, in terms of their potential scores on the independent variables for measuring learning. Therefore, replication of this study would be essential to substantiate its findings.
- *Total sample size was 210, with 147 completing the questionnaires*: This level of attrition could be a concern, but the researchers provide an explanation for this, and the total size is still acceptable for power of the subsequent inferential analysis.

Morling et al. (2008)

- *Quasi-experimental, mixed factorial design*: Students were allocated to the experimental groupings (class groups). Therefore, in spite of the random nature of this process, the design was not truly experimental. Two lecturers used (a and b, independent groups), two modes of engagement (clicker versus traditional, independent groups) and four different exams (student exam results across the semester, repeated measures).
- *Total sample size was 1290 students*: This is a large sample, which is more than sufficient for the analysis completed. Reference is made that the final analysis was based on complete data across the semester, but no figure of student attrition was provided.

Analysis: methods for interpreting data

With effective planning of your project, you will have a clear conception of how the variables measured interact. The analysis should present a succinct expression of the evidence for your research hypotheses. A common mistake is when researchers try to present too much, giving the impression that they have simply mined the dataset for opportunistic findings, which might be spurious. As in other research areas, the type of analysis conducted will influence the conclusions that can be drawn from the data collected, and therefore your ability to make a contribution to the knowledge base in this area. By referencing previous papers in the area and looking at what forms of analysis are appropriate, you can see what is needed to convey your findings.

Once you have completed the data analysis, your attention will turn to the presentation of the findings. While each journal will have specific guidelines and accepted norms regarding the presentation of results, and these should be followed, there is a logical sequence to be followed, which reflects the hierarchy of enquiry you have adopted:

1 Data preparation: data transformation, truncation, missing data and exclusions
2 Descriptive statistics: measures of central tendency, measures of spread, measures of normality
3 Inferential statistics: parametric or non-parametric tests and post-hoc follow-up tests
4 Figures: plots and graphs
5 Summary: written summation of key findings.

Azzawi and Dawson (2007)

- Descriptive exploration of evaluations using percentages and bar charts, examining differences between the student groups
- Percentage of hits for each of the intranet elements
- Descriptive exploration of summative assessment performance differences between the student groups
- Correlation analysis of A-level performance and assessment performance.

The analysis completed explored each of the elements and is presented in a logical order. However, some conventions have not been followed. The information gained from the intranet is presented as percentage hits, but this is not broken down further to see what type of students accessed the information. If this had been feasible, it would have been extremely useful. One of the bar graphs contains asterisks that denote significant differences between two groups. In the text, the full results of these t-tests should have been reported.

Choi and Johnson (2006)

- A mixed factorial ANOVA was conducted with post-hoc t-tests.

The inferential analyses completed are logical in order and most of the essential information is contained. The written commentary highlights the key issues. There is, however, no descriptive analysis of the data, and therefore it is difficult to know where the scores are placed on the continuous scales of satisfaction, comprehension and retention, how far group scores varied from these central scores, and if the distribution had significant skew or kurtosis.

Morling et al. (2008)

- Descriptive and inferential exploration of differences in each exam results for the clicker and traditional groups are provided
- Descriptive and inferential exploration of differences in interest and engagement by lecturer group are provided
- A further inferential analysis of interaction between clicker use and student achievement (comparison of high achieving and low achieving students) on exam scores.

There are number of components to this analysis, and these involve complex interaction effects. This is achievable because of the large sample size. Exam score and engagement are presented as separate sections, which assists the reader in navigating through the information.

Concluding thoughts

Early planning of any study is essential and will greatly enhance your ability to foresee potential complications and work them out before you get to the point where there is no going back. It is essential that you remain focused on what your primary objective is, rather than trying to do too much. Familiarize yourself with the peer reviewed publications in your area. You may find these in disciplinary journals, general higher education journals or journals on the scholarship of teaching and learning in higher education.

Critically examine how other colleagues have constructed studies, measured variables, performed analyses and presented their findings. Examining exemplars will ground you in the achievable and help you to create a plan of action.

Start with the familiar. Think about your own practice – how you can strategically measure the impact of changes in your teaching on student learning and outcomes. Use your background in scientific and quantitative methodology to your advantage to shape and inform your practice as an academic.

12

Combining qualitative and quantitative: mixed-methods in small-scale research

Sarah Skerratt

Introduction to mixed methods research

Two earlier chapters focused on methods for carrying out small-scale research projects on teaching and learning in higher education: Chapter 10 described qualitative tools and processes, and Chapter 11 described quantitative approaches. This chapter on combined methods explores ways of combining quantitative and qualitative frameworks and analyses and reviews the strengths of a 'mixed' approach.

Reasons for mixed methods

For two types of inquiry a mixed methods approach is particularly useful:

1 when the problem you want to study is multi-faceted and therefore requires multiple perspectives from a range of disciplines, each of which has its own tools and approaches
2 when you want to carry out a multi-stage piece of research, which goes either from in-depth (individual) to macro-(population) level or, conversely, from an analysis of trends in a larger sample down to the behaviour, attitudes and perceptions of a small sub-set of the population.

If your small-scale research project idea falls into either of these categories, then it is worth considering mixed methods as a way forward for your investigation.

The multi-faceted research problem

Investigating teaching and learning involves problems or issues that have many aspects; some will be more amenable to statistical analyses, others to in-depth qualitative investigation, and rigorous analysis arguably requires 'dialogue' between quantitative and qualitative datasets.

For example, if you want to find out whether student experiences of distance learning lead to isolation from peers, you may want to explore specific aspects of this subject through an online questionnaire, using prompts and ideas from the literature. You may want to focus on specific quantifiable aspects of 'isolation', such as the number of times (frequency) one student contacts another student; which topics are discussed; which tasks prompt lone working; which tasks prompt collaborative working; percentage of time spent networking; percentage of online time spent in peer-to-peer contact. These could be seen as 'indicators' of the existence and extent of isolation.

You may then wish to complement this part of your investigation with an approach that gives students the opportunity to describe 'isolation', using their own terminology, or their own tell-tale signs, and you may also encourage them to identify the implications, the 'So what?' of isolation for their learning experience. In this context, a qualitative approach is appropriate. This could include offline interviews and/or focus group discussions when these distance learning students come together for their summer school or other annual workshop.

Combining tools in this way creates a richer picture, and the inquiry is more exciting, because each approach yields different data types, which are part of the whole.

Furthermore, these types of inquiry (quantitative and qualitative) can be cyclical, with feedback loops built in to the research design and research procedures (see Figure 12.1):

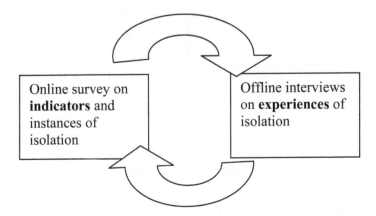

Figure 12.1 A cyclical approach to gathering data through mixed methods

This approach enables complementary aspects of the picture to be generated, checked and rechecked. It also allows for 'participant validation', where findings can be presented back to those who provided the responses, to check that the researcher has understood what the interviewees intended. This cyclical approach is based on an understanding that the topic of study is complex, requires a multi-method investigation, as well as the opportunity to review data and its interpretation, including review with participants or the 'subjects' of the study.

The multi-stage research inquiry process

A step-by-step inquiry process can lead to an incremental growth in understanding the research problem or topic, as each stage is designed, implemented and completed. One stage is designed to feed into the next, with the later stages being dependent on the earlier ones, and comprehension being built up over time.

In cases where you are not sure of the extent to which a particular (educational and learning) practice is successful, and also where you are not sure of the range of issues that will be relevant to your topic, this approach is extremely useful, because it gives you the chance to refine your ideas during the research process.

There are two routes for mixing methods in this sequential way: (1) from quantitative to qualitative; and (2) from qualitative to quantitative, as shown in Figure 12.2.

(1) From quantitative to qualitative		(2) From qualitative to quantitative	
Data collection activity	**Tools and approaches**	**Data collection activity**	**Tools and approaches**
Survey of population (e.g. all students on a campus)	Survey questionnaire Closed questions **Quantitative** data	In-depth interviews with purposive sample of individuals Observation also possible	Semi-structured interview format **Qualitative**, textual and observational data
Focus groups of sub-samples	Semi-structured interview format **Qualitative**, textual and observational data	Focus groups where ideas from individual interviews are explored	Semi-structured interview format **Qualitative**, textual and observational data
Face to face interviews with (i) individuals from focus groups and (ii) other stakeholders	Semi-structured interview format **Qualitative**, textual information	Large-scale survey to examine extent to which views or behaviours are expressed more widely	Survey questionnaire Closed questions **Quantitative** data

Figure 12.2 Step by step, mixed methods research processes

From quantitative to qualitative

You can begin with a questionnaire survey to a large number of respondents (see Chapter 11 for important sampling and design issues), and this enables you to scope out the issues you are examining. This is often called the 'scoping phase' of the research. It allows you to generate data that give you an impression of the overall landscape. This is also described as taking the 'helicopter view', before you select where to go next in your inquiry.

The next two stages comprise further degrees of refining your research – use focus groups to present findings from the survey (see Chapter 10 for a description of group interviews). You can either present the findings at the beginning of the discussion, in order to gauge respondents' views on them, or you can give respondents an opportunity to express their views, while they are unaware of the survey findings, and then present the findings to them to see what they think. Choice of approach depends on whether you want simply to check what they think of the survey findings, or also to compare findings from two different 'disclosure settings' (Skerratt, 2008). (Disclosure settings are the contexts in which individuals give their responses. Questionnaires are one setting, group interviews are other settings. It is possible that interviewees will respond differently according to these contexts, primarily in relation to whether their responses are private or public.)

The third step is where you go into greater depth on some or all of the topics addressed in the survey and focus groups, to investigate 'why' the findings from the earlier phases might have occurred (see Chapter 10 for a description of interviewing). This, therefore, is a process whereby you create a funnel down which you travel, becoming more and more focused on a specific set of issues, as if increasing the magnification at every step.

From qualitative to quantitative

Conversely, the second option begins at the ground level and ends with the overall landscape view. The purpose of the first phase is, again, to scope out the field of inquiry. This time, however, the starting point is an in-depth examination of opinions, thoughts, behaviours, words used/not used and people's underpinning rationale, enjoying the discovery of all the layers of complexity and exploring the extent to which patterns of thought or behaviour exist amongst your sample of interviewees (see Chapter 10 for qualitative sampling options).

Having analysed these findings, you can then examine the extent to which they are repeated among a range of different people, this time in a different disclosure setting. That is, are there views that are only privately held? Are there views and behaviours that are also permissible to discuss, in certain ways, amongst peers, colleagues, friends? How are things discussed? Which words are used / not used, and how do people react to certain norms or ideas about teaching and learning? In this way, you are looking at the extent to which group settings lead to contrasts with the types of data you generated from the one-to-one interview phase.

Finally, if you want to examine the extent to which your findings resonate in a wider population, or, conversely, if you find that they are particular to the people you interviewed individually and in the groups, you can gather a different type of data which will complement the 'thick' (Patton, 1986) material you already have. In this way you can look for patterns of repeatability. You can also look for representativeness of those views through statistically robust approaches (see Chapter 11).

Feedback loops

It is also possible, as with the multi-faceted approach outlined above, to create feedback loops, so that not only does one stage feed onto the next, but, once you have reached the end of the first cycle, you can begin again, refining your investigation through several cycles, as described in Figures 12.3 and 12.4.

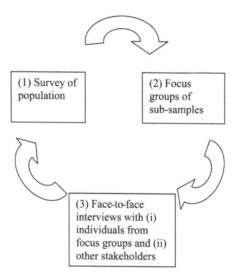

| (1) Survey of population | (2) Focus groups of sub-samples |

(3) Face-to-face interviews with (i) individuals from focus groups and (ii) other stakeholders

Figure 12.3 Step-by-step quantitative to qualitative approach

What can mixed methods tell you?

A mixed methods approach brings the strengths of both qualitative and quantitative inquiry to your small-scale research project. Combining these methods, rather than relying on the strengths of one, can produce the following benefits (Table 12.1).

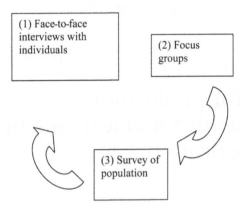

Figure 12.4 Step-by-step qualitative to quantitative approach

Table 12.1 Combined strengths of quantitative and qualitative inquiry

Quantitative – strengths	Qualitative – strengths
Allows you to generate data about what people do, whether and how often it is repeated, and the incidence in a population	Allows you to generate data about why people think and behave as they do, and the reported implications of their perceptions and behaviours
Lets you test how significant your findings are amongst a wide population, through rigorous sampling and analysis of data	Lets you investigate the 'messiness' and variability in the range and diversity of responses from individual and group interviews

Concluding comment

If your proposed research project or idea is either multi-faceted or requires multiple steps to investigate it, then a mixed methods approach could be useful and could add strength and value to your data, your findings and what you are able to say based on your investigation. The key is to ensure that your choice of methods is appropriate to the questions you want to address – think first of your aim, objectives, hypotheses or research question(s), and then examine the range of approaches open to you.

13

Writing for publication about teaching and learning in higher education

Rowena Murray

Introduction: beyond 'show-and-tell'

Whatever definition is given to the word 'scholarship' – and there will be many – publication can be part of it. Taking ideas to a public forum, where they can be subjected to peer review, is an essential part of scholarship. Being active in SoTL therefore involves writing for peer-reviewed journals, in your discipline's journals and/or in SoTL/higher education journals.

When lecturers start reading higher education journals there is an initial culture shock. They are often surprised, challenged – some are even appalled – by the contrast between the methods, concepts and definitions of 'research' used in their disciplines' journals and those in higher education journals.

When they start writing for higher education journals, some of these disciplinary differences raise searching, legitimate questions: What constitutes research in SoTL, or in a specific journal? What makes research in a specific journal robust? What constitutes new knowledge in that journal? The simplest answer to these questions is that higher education journals have moved beyond descriptive accounts of innovation. 'Show-and-tell' is no longer enough.

This chapter explores journals using examples of published papers, selected not in order to promote a specific type of research, scholarship or writing, but to illustrate the options open to writers. Before that, there are practical strategies for academics moving from their disciplines to write in SoTL and higher education.

Targeting a higher education journal

I have written elsewhere (Murray, 2005) about analysing higher education journals for their focus, context, mode of argument, structure, etc. Writers can scope out target journals by looking for standard cues:

1 Read the journal's description of its aims and the types of papers required
2 Review several recent issues of the journal
3 Focus on the usual key areas: titles, topics, methodologies, data types, types of contribution to knowledge etc.
4 Select a few papers, or at least, one, of the type you want to write, or the type suited to the work you have done.

For each of the papers selected, a more detailed analysis helps writers who are new to writing about SoTL develop a sense of what is required:

- How is the paper's contribution articulated?
- Does it appear in the last sentence of the abstract?
- How is it elaborated towards the end of the paper?
- How is this claim to contribution evidenced?
- What literature contextualizes both problem/inquiry and findings?

This analysis helps academics from different disciplines develop a sense of what 'research' means in SoTL.

Having scoped out the journal, you can contact the editor to check that your idea for your paper is appropriate. Some editors encourage this, because such inquiries let them screen contributions, and this saves them time. It also lets you check not only that your analysis of the journal is accurate, but also that the journal you have chosen is not about to drop your topic. This saves you wasting time writing a paper for the 'wrong' journal. Your initial inquiry can be a short email:

Email subject
Studies in Higher Education: Initial inquiry

Email content
I am writing a paper about [subject of your paper] ...
This paper [what you say about that subject] ...
This paper could/would be of interest to readers of *Studies in Higher Education* because ...
Do you think this would be appropriate?

Clearly, there are many ways to write this type of enquiry, and some will think it an odd step to take, even though many editors welcome it. Some writers prefer to send a draft abstract, but that has a different purpose from finding out if a paper's subject is appropriate for a specific journal. In addition, draft abstracts require editors to read more, which they may not want to do.

When editors respond to this type of enquiry – usually promptly – their comments range from the very general: 'This sounds like the kind of thing for our journal, but it would, of course, be subject to peer review ...'; to the more specific: 'Our journal would be interested in this paper if you could emphasize ... rather than ...' This kind of comment is extremely useful, as it helps writers adjust the focus of their papers in ways that are appropriate for the journals they are targeting. Of course, writers who decide that they cannot make the requested adjustments to their papers can target other journals, again saving time for editors and themselves.

Examples

Papers discussed in this section were selected to illustrate the range of definitions of 'research' and 'scholarship' in SoTL. All of these papers have been judged to be about more than 'show-and-tell', in other words, they are more than simply descriptive. All of them – different as they are – were judged to have made a contribution to the field.

This is not to say that there will not be debates about criteria that appear to have been used – clearly there will be debates between academics about terminology and standards in SoTL, as in other disciplines. Neither are these examples presented as ideal models. However, they illustrate the care with which we calculate the impact of an intervention in higher education teaching and learning. The last two examples, in the last section of this chapter, show authors publishing on SoTL in their own disciplines.

Literature reviews/background/context

Just as the word 'research' has new meanings for academics moving into writing about SoTL, the terms 'method', 'data' and 'contribution' will be defined in new ways in this discipline. In fact, with such a range of approaches, even a literature review can serve a range of purposes and may be written in different ways.

In one example, the journal required almost no literature review, and what little there was appeared in the abstract:

> Online web tools are becoming an important and accessible means of supporting learning in higher education. Student writing is central to teaching and learning (Lillis, 2001). This paper describes an online tool designed to support student dissertation writing. By combining three types of online space – instructional material, a writing space and planning templates – this tool aimed to provide a holistic approach to writing and writing development. This paper demonstrates how the tool was used in an academic course in order to address certain teaching and learning problems identified by the course tutor. Student feedback suggests that while further development is needed, the tool was still useful. This paper raises awareness of the complex array of issues involved in dissertation

writing and provides insights into solutions to writing problems. While we designed what we considered to be a web-based tool for dissertation writing, we argue that the writing space and planning templates go some way towards creating an environment for the development of learning (Häkinen, 2002) (Strachan et al., 2004).

For this type of paper – known as a 'colloquium' in the *British Journal of Educational Technology* – this was an appropriate way to establish the study's context.

A more standard, detailed literature review (Morss and Murray, 2001) takes up one and a half printed pages, beginning with a quotation establishing the dearth of literature on the paper's subject, academics' writing: 'The British literature on the academic writing role is similar to that on research: patchy' (Blaxter et al., 1998: 290). This is followed by a list of references to books designed to support academics' writing, then more detail – a paragraph each – on four key researchers in this field, who take different approaches to the subject.

As in other disciplines, the literature review can represent different approaches in the literature in the form of a debate about the subject. For example, a paper on the doctoral examination (or 'viva') represented the literature as a debate centred on problems it poses for students:

> A wide-ranging literature informs us of the tensions, ambiguities and recurring questions about the viva [three references]. Interviews, scholarly analyses and student surveys indicate the root causes of such problems [three references]. Severe scrutiny of the doctoral experience in general, and of the viva in particular, is not confined to the UK [one reference]. Perhaps, however, it is time to move beyond the generation of tensions and questions in order to consider how students, supervisors and examiners could prepare, strategically and/or tactically, for the viva experience. (Murray, 2003: 109)

Alternatively, the literature review can have more than one function. In the following example the first literature review establishes the need for an intervention, a writing consultation. The second presents an intervention originating in another discipline, with its own literature:

> It could be argued that all academics with good first degrees and higher degrees will have developed the ability to write for scholarly publication. However, this assumption was questioned as long ago as 1987, when Boice established that becoming an academic writer can be challenging, and attempting to increase written output can present significant problems ... Moreover, changes in the aims, culture and management of higher education bring new demands on academics' time ... These changes can impinge on academics' time for research and academic writing [four references].

Many factors may be associated with an academics' inability to find writing time [two references], and there are many potential solutions to the problem [seven references]. (Murray et al., 2008: 119–20)

The second literature review defines 'recognised … strategies' (p. 120) from another discipline that could be adapted to support academic writing:

Research on behaviour change in other domains offers potential models and concepts [two references].

This research has established that behaviour change requires more than acquisition of new knowledge [two references]…

One model for enabling behaviour change has particular relevance for academic writers … [two references], and research shows that this type of consultation leads to behaviour change [three references]. (Murray et al., 2008: 121)

In addition, this paper references recent changes in the structure, financing and management of higher education: increasing student numbers, widening access, demand for student support, accountability and administration, income generation and continuing professional development, to which could be added pressure to develop innovative approaches to teaching and learning. The case is made that all of these potentially impinge on academic writing. This argument is put in an international context by references to literature on academic writing in several higher education cultures: USA, Australia and the UK.

There are similarities and differences between literature reviews in SoTL and in other disciplines. However, this section shows the range within SoTL and higher education journals: from almost no literature review, to two sections reviewing two sets of literature from different disciplines. There is a similar range of options for other sections of papers published in this field.

Methods

With a subject as complex as education, evaluating an intervention is going to be complex. Any claim for impact – on student learning or performance, for example – must be evidenced. As with any discipline, the methods chosen must suit the research aims. In evaluations, multiple forms of information can go some way to capturing the complexity. For example, assessing the impact of a writing for publication programme on academics involved gathering different types of data at different times:

The aims of this research … were to track and monitor individuals on the programme in terms of their original goals from the outset, their interim goals and progress, their written output and their perceptions of the benefits in terms of soft outcomes. We attempted to capture the complexity by using several evaluation strategies. Hard output was measured by asking participants to list their completed work: articles accepted by refereed journals, refereed conference papers accepted, books chapters, and other writing projects completed ... This output was matched against pre-programme goals. (Morss and Murray, 2001: 40)

In this study, data on 'soft' outcomes – for example, confidence – were gathered using four measures: discussions at meetings, monitoring form, questionnaire and focus group. Each was explained in a short section of the paper. Results were presented in table form, with one table presenting themes generated in all the evaluative strategies. Two pages were given to discussion, in which different interpretations of the findings were considered. This section used the authors' experience in this area as a point of reference: 'Our interpretation is that confidence is the key, but our experience tells us that building confidence in this context involves several functions; one of these functions alone might not have impact' (Morss and Murray, 2001: 49).

A potential weakness in the study was identified: participants were self-selecting, limiting the extent to which we could generalize from findings (not that this type of study lends itself to generalization). However, this limitation was offset with a strength: the wide range of experiences, length of service and academic disciplines in the group studied.

Multiple methods also featured in the article on a Web-based tool for dissertation writers: a questionnaire to students about their views on and use of the website, a focus group with students to explore their points in more depth and the tutor's perspective on the impact of the site on students.

Data/results/outcomes

Examples in this chapter show that data is presented in different ways in publications in this field: there is a spectrum from detailed to general. Analysis of data in this type of work is reported in ways that may seem to academics from other disciplines as 'sketchy': 'Perspectives of the students and tutor are summarized below ... Two key topics were raised [by the tutor]' (Strachan et al., 2004: 373–4).

Data can consist of recurring student questions or persistent problems in a specific teaching context, drawing on the lecturer's observations or analysis of student discussion or performance. These can be distilled down to a core set of issues that, taken together, identify student learning needs:

This paper draws on viva preparation workshops conducted at the University of Strathclyde and at other universities in the UK. In workshop discussions, students' questions reveal anxieties, expectations and gaps in their understanding of the viva. A comprehensive list of questions would suggest that every aspect of the viva is unknown to students. However, analysis reveals recurring issues and underlying ambiguities in the viva. Given that universities provide so much information to students, it is surprising that students have so many questions. However, students' questions do not indicate ignorance, but show them positioning the viva as a new communication event. The implications of this analysis for the viva are that a panel of examiners, rather than national standards, might provide the foundation for transparency, and rhetorical development, rather than more information, would enhance students' and supervisors' understandings and preparations. (Murray, 2003: 109)

This paper is descriptive rather than empirical. However, there is a dataset: observations were collected over more than ten years, and students' recurring questions were identified.

At the other end of the spectrum is the paper with multiple datasets (Morss and Murray, 2001): 29 topics raised by writers at discussions are listed (table II, p. 40); ten writers' pre-programme goals are listed in one column, alongside their achievements in a second column (table III, p. 41); six themes derived from all evaluative strategies in this study are synthesized (table IV, p. 42).

By comparison, the paper on the Web-based tool for dissertation writers, while it makes an equally strong case for the intervention, has much less detail on data:

Student perspective

Students reported that they used the site 'once' or 'occasionally'. They did not use the site throughout the entire dissertation process. However, all students who had looked at the site, and those students who had used it, found it to be useful ...

Tutor perspective

Two key topics were raised: (a) the educational impact of the site and (b) the students' ability to plan their dissertations using the tool

(Strachan et al., 2004: 373–4)

Whatever our assessments of what constitutes data in the studies reported in these papers, it is important to acknowledge that they were published. This is not to say that they all represent ground-breaking research – not all research is ground-breaking. Each study made a contribution in some sense, and in the course of writing these papers the authors will have increased their knowledge and enhanced their practice.

Contributions

These papers made different types of contribution. The spectrum stretches from evidenced benefits of an intervention to potential benefits of a concept. Both have the potential to shape knowledge and practice. With such a wide range, authors have to distinguish how much – or how little – to claim as a contribution. As in other disciplines, contribution is bounded, or delimited, and relative to other work, usually referenced explicitly at those points in the paper – generally in the conclusions – where authors claim their contributions.

For example, the dissertation writing-tool paper identified both recorded and potential benefits of the intervention. The website created an environment for a specific type of learning, and for some students – and for the tutor – this had benefits. For part-time students, of which there were many on this course, this intervention was an important improvement in the course. However, while the study achieved its aims, there were limitations: the authors identify improvements that could be made to the site and to the process of embedding the tool in the course.

By contrast, where there is very little published work on a topic, establishing a concept or principle may be a project – and a paper – in itself. For example, the paper on students' questions about the viva established that it could be seen as a new type of 'communication event'.

Similarly, the writing consultation paper had neither method nor data in the conventional sense, although it tells us that the approach was trialled with academics. The purpose of this paper was not to 'evidence' but to 'describe', 'analyse', 'propose' and 'demonstrate' how a new approach might be adopted:

> This article *describes* and *analyses* a specific mechanism, the writing consultation, designed to help academics to prioritise, reconceptualise and improve their writing practices. It makes the case for its potential to stimulate consideration of writing practices and motivations, a possible precondition for creating time for writing in academic contexts. This article *proposes* that the process of revealing and developing writing practices in a specific form of regular, structured, collegial discussion has potential to prompt academics to reconceptualise their writing practices and, perhaps crucially, to find different ways to write. In addition, it *demonstrates*, in a new way, how recognised behaviour change strategies might be embedded in the academic writing process. The writing consultation draws on principles established in other contexts. This article makes the case for adapting them to the context

of academic writing, in order to support and improve academic writing output. [my emphasis] (Murray et al., 2008: 119)

The claim to contribution was carefully crafted: 'The approach proposed in this article involved looking for more established theory in other areas for insights that might have relevance in this important but under-researched area ... The writing consultation could be one way of providing the "structured interventions" that McGrail, Rickard, and Jones (2006) recommend' (Murray et al., 2008: 124). McGrail et al.'s (2006) systematic review of interventions to improve academic writing cited the Morss and Murray (2001) paper, suggesting that its claim to contribution was valid:

> This paper provides data on what writers do ... We have also described processes for finding out more about what writers do ... Barriers to writing and strategies for overcoming them have been identified. The research also reveals the complexity of writing and writing development. (Morss and Murray, 2001: 50)

In some of these papers, the contributions seem modest. This can be attributed to the difficulty of establishing – and evidencing – new concepts and behaviours, and capturing – or distinguishing – variables brought into play when academics and students change the way they learn and work.

SoTL in the discipline

In addition to SoTL and higher education journals, there are journals that either include or focus on education in specific disciplines. Two examples in this section, one from a science journal (*Physiotherapy*) and the other from a social science journal (*Legal Studies*), show how SoTL can be integrated in the disciplines.

For a scientific journal, studies are likely to be more evidence-based. For example, an evaluation of a writing for publication course gathered evidence in interviews:

> This paper describes an example of a writing for publication course, and reports on an evaluation of the long-term outcomes of the course for participating allied health professionals. The main purpose of the study was to explore the mechanisms involved in scholarly publication. It was particularly important to assess the extent to which participants used practices they had developed on the course when they returned to the workplace. Their publication rate was also identified. (Murray and Newton, 2008: 30)

What was new about this paper – and it was important to make this explicit in this scientific journal – was that it was 'the first to examine the writing behaviour of clinical allied health professionals' (p. 32).

In this study data consisted of interview transcripts, which were subjected to qualitative analysis. Participants' accounts of their practices, their statements about what they learned on the course and their outputs after the course were used to construct an argument about writing practices likely to lead to success in publication.

Information about their actual published outputs added a quantitative element to the study. In addition, the study used participants' accounts of persistent barriers to writing for publication in the workplace to raise questions about how writing should be managed in professional settings.

Although this was an education topic, the paper was designated as an 'expert article' in this journal. Because it was written for a scientific journal, this paper used more features of scientific style than the examples discussed above, including features of scientific reporting:

> One year after the end of the course, participants were contacted and invited to take part in a semi-structured interview. The tape-recorded interview lasted for approximately 45 minutes. The tapes were transcribed verbatim and verified with participants. The transcriptions were coded, and emergent themes were identified and checked by an independent researcher. (Murray and Newton, 2008: 31)

As for other scientific studies reported in this journal, the paper confirmed that the study was approved by the formal process of the local health service ethics committee. The paper concluded with reflections on the study's implications for the Physiotherapy curriculum and the management of writing for publication in clinical workplaces.

The *Legal Studies* article also looked at academic work, specifically the use of sabbaticals in Law Schools:

> This paper attempts to contribute to the increasing body of research on the working practices of legal academics and what has been called the 'private life' of the law school. It seeks to subject to further empirical investigation the analysis made by ... It examines one under-researched aspect of academic practice, namely the award of sabbaticals ... The paper reviews the relevant literature on sabbaticals, reports on the results of a study of the published criteria law schools have for awarding sabbaticals and analyses responses to a questionnaire sent to law school heads on the operation of their policies ... [The use of sabbaticals] impacts on the formation of the professional identities of legal academics. Those who are excluded from this benefit may be marginalised and areas of academic labour considered inappropriate for sabbaticals consequently regarded as secondary. This may entrench already existing areas of inequality. (Spencer and Kent, 2007: 649)

The methodology adopted was an examination of published criteria used by universities to award sabbaticals. The second stage was a questionnaire survey of heads of law schools, focusing on sabbatical awards over a three-year period. Survey findings are presented in terms of practices, availability, academic work deemed appropriate for sabbaticals, profiles of staff taking sabbaticals and gender. Questionnaire findings are reported in terms of management of sabbaticals, including rejection rates, the Research Assessment Exercise and the use of sabbaticals for 'reflection rather than production' (p. 669). The authors conclude with an extended discussion of issues raised by the study, including the finding that sabbaticals play a part in the pressure to publish:

> [Sabbaticals'] link with teaching in the old universities particularly, but to some extent across the sector as a whole, is not clearly enunciated and it does not appear that a specific influence on pedagogy is an expected outcome. Rather, the pre-occupation with research en- trenches the message that teaching, and thus by implication staff more closely involved in teaching, are marginal. (Spencer and Kent, 2007: 671)

As in the previous sections of this chapter, these two examples convey the range of types of work and writing that can be carried out in SoTL and higher education. Unlike the other examples, these two show how features of the discipline shape the work and writing.

Conclusion

This chapter shows the range of topics to write about in SoTL, including undergraduate learning and teaching, postgraduate learning and supervi- sion, and academic work and skills. It shows different ways of going beyond 'show-and-tell'.

When discussing papers published in SoTL and higher education jour- nals, academics from other disciplines tend to re-evaluate the papers, questioning the standards applied by the journals or reviewers in this discipline. However, whatever views we may have on the relative strengths of these papers, we have to acknowledge that they were all judged to be adequate for publication in these journals at the time of publication. As the literature matures, standards may indeed change, but analysing what 're- search' and 'scholarship' mean for a specific type of work, for a specific journal at a specific time should probably remain part of lecturers' prepara- tion for publishing on SoTL and higher education.

Bibliography

Airey, D. and Tribe, J. (2000) Education for Hospitality, in C. Lashley and A. Morrison (eds) *In Search of Hospitality*. Oxford: Butterworth Heinemann.

Åkerlind, G.S. (2008) Growing and developing as a university researcher, *Higher Education*, 55: 241–54.

Amey, M.J. and Brown, D.F. (2005) Interdisciplinary collaboration and academic work: a case study of a university – community partnership, in E.G. Creamer and L.R. Lettuca (eds) *Advancing Faculty Learning through Interdisciplinary Collaboration*. New Directions in Teaching and Learning no.102. San Francisco: Jossey-Bass.

Anderson, C. and Day, K. (2005) Purposive environments: engaging students in the values and practices of history, *Higher Education*, 49: 319–43.

Andresen, L.W. (2000) A useable, trans-disciplinary conception of scholarship, *Higher Education Research and Development*, 19(2): 137–53.

Angelo, T. (ed.) (1991) *New Directions for Teaching and Learning*, no. 46. San Francisco: Jossey-Bass.

Angelo, T. (ed.) (1998) *New Directions for Teaching and Learning*. San Francisco: Jossey-Bass.

Angelo, T. (1999) Doing assessment as if learning matters most, *AAHE Bulletin*.

Astin, A. et al. (1995) Nine principles of good practice for assessing student learning, *Assessment Forum*, American Association of Higher Education (AAHE). www.aahe.org/assessment/principl.htm

Azzawi, M. and Dawson, M.M. (2007) The effectiveness of lecture-integrated, web-supported case studies in large group teaching, *Bioscience Education eJournal*, 10.

Barnett, R. (1990) *The Idea of Higher Education*. Buckingham: Open University Press/SRHE

Barnett, R. (1997) *Higher Education: A Critical Business*. Buckingham: Open University Press/SRHE.

Barnett, R. (2007) *A Will to Learn*. Maidenhead: Open University Press/SRHE.

Barr, R. and Tagg, J. (1995) From teaching to learning: A new paradigm for undergraduate education, *Change*, Nov./Dec. 13–25.

Bass, R. (1998–99) The scholarship of teaching: what's the problem? *Inventio*, 1998–99, online journal. www.doiiit.gmu.edu/inventio/randybass.htm.

Bassey, M. (1999) *Case Study Research in Educational Settings*. Buckingham: Open University Press.

Bateson, J.E.G. and Hoffman, K.D. (1999) *Managing Services Marketing*, 4th edn. Fort Worth: Dryden Press.

Baynham, M. (2000) Academic writing in new and emergent discipline areas, in M.R. Lea and B. Stierer (eds) *Student Writing in Higher Education: New Contexts*. Buckingham: Open University Press/SRHE.

Becher, T. (1989) *Academic Tribes and Territories: Intellectual Enquiry and the Culture of Disciplines*. Buckingham: Open University Press/SRHE.

Becher, T. and Trowler, P. (2001) *Academic Tribes and Territories: Intellectual Enquiry and the Culture of Disciplines*, 2nd edn. Buckingham: Open University Press/SRHE.

Bentz, V. M. and Shapiro, J. J. (1998) *Mindful Inquiry in Social Research*. Thousand Oaks, CA: Sage.

Bernstein, B. (1996) *Pedagogy, Symbolic Control and Identity.* London: Taylor & Francis.

Bernstein, D.J., Nelson, A., Goodburn, A. and Savory, P. (2006) *Making Teaching and Learning Visible: Course Portfolios and the Peer Review of Teaching.* San Francisco: Jossey-Bass/Anker.

Biggs, J. (2003) *Teaching for Quality Learning at University: What the Student Does,* 2nd edn. Maidenhead: Open University Press/SRHE.

Biggs, J. and Tang, C. (2007) *Teaching for Quality Learning at University,* 3rd edn. Maidenhead: Open University Press/SRHE.

Biglan, A. (1973) Relationships between subject matter characteristics and the structure and output of university departments, *Journal of Applied Psychology,* 57: 204–13.

Blackler, F. (1995) Knowledge, knowledge work and organizations: a overview and interpretation, in D. Hickson and S. Clegg (eds) *Organisation Studies,* 6: 1021–46.

Blackler, F. and Crump, N. (2000) Organizing processes in complex activity networks, *Organization,* 7(2): 277–300.

Blaxter, L, Hughes, C. and Tight, M. (1998) Writing on academic careers, *Studies in Higher Education,* 23: 281–95.

Bloom, D. (ed.) (1956) *Taxonomy of Educational Objectives: Book 1, The Cognitive Domain.* London: Longman.

Boden, R. (2005) *Academic's Support Kit.* London: Sage.

Boice, R. (1987) Is released time an effective component of faculty development programs? *Research in Higher Education,* 26: 311–26.

Bolton, G. (2005) *Reflective Practice: Writing and Professional Development,* 2nd edn. London: Sage.

Boston, C. (2002) The concept of formative assessment, *ERIC Digest* (ED 470 206). College Park, Maryland: ERIC Clearinghouse on Assessment and Evaluation. www.ericfacility.net/databases/ERIC_Digests/ed470206.html

Boud, D. (1986) *Implementing Student Self-Assessment.* Kensington, NSW: Higher Education Research and Development Society of Australia (HERSDA).

Bowden, J. and Marton, F. (1998) *The University of Learning: Beyond Quality and Competence in Higher Education.* London: Kogan Page.

Boyd, P., Harris, K. and Murray, J. (2007) *Becoming a Teacher Educator: Guidelines for the Induction of Newly Appointed Lecturers in Initial Teacher Education.* http://escalate.ac.uk/3662 (accessed 12th May 2008).

Boyer, E. (1990) *Scholarship Reconsidered: Priorities of the Professoriate.* San Francisco, CA: Jossey-Bass.

Braxton, J.M., and Toombs, W. (1982) Faculty uses of doctoral training: consideration of a technique for the differentiation of scholarly effort from research activity, *Research in Higher Education,* 16: 265–82.

Brems, C., Baldwin, M., Davis, L. and Namyniuk, L. (1994) The impostor syndrome as related to teaching evaluations and advising relationships of university faculty members, *The Journal of Higher Education,* 65(2): 183–93.

Brew, A. (2006) *Research and Teaching: Beyond the Divide.* London: Palgrave MacMillan.

Brew, A. (2007) Imperatives and challenges in integrating research and teaching: a case study. Background paper for Carrick Institute for Learning and Teaching in Higher Education Discipline-Based Development Forum: Teaching/Research Nexus, Adelaide, 29–30 August.

Brockbank, A. and McGill, I. (2007) *Facilitating Reflective Learning in Higher Education*, 2nd edn. Buckingham: Open University Press/SRHE.

Brookfield, S. (2005) *Discussion as a Way of Teaching: Tools and Techniques for University Teachers*, 2nd edn. New Jersey: Jossey-Bass.

Brotherton, B. and Wood, R. (2000) Hospitality and Hospitality Management, in C. Lashley and A. Morrison (eds) *In Search of Hospitality: Theoretical Perspectives and Debates*. Oxford: Butterworth Heinemann.

Brown, S. and Knight, P. (1994) *Assessing Learners in Higher Education*. London: Kogan Page.

Bryan, C. and Clegg, K. (2007) (eds) *Innovative Assessment in Higher Education*. London: Routledge.

Cannon, R. and Newble, D. (2002) *A Handbook for Teachers in Universities and Colleges: A Guide to Improving Teaching Methods*. London: Kogan Page.

Carlile, O. and Jordan, A. (2007) Reflective writing: principles and practice, in C. O'Farrell (ed.) *Teaching Portfolio Practice in Ireland: A Handbook*. Dublin: CAPSL and All Ireland Society for Higher Education in Ireland.

Castles, J. (2004) Persistence and the adult learner: factors affecting persistence in Open University students, *Active Learning in Higher Education*, 5(2): 166–79.

Cerbin, W. (2000) Investigating student learning in a problem-based psychology course, *Opening lines: Approaches to the scholarship of teaching and learning*. Menlo Park, CA: The Carnegie Foundation for the Advancement of Teaching.

Chickering, A. and Gamson, Z. (1987) Seven Principles of Good Practice in Undergraduate Education, *AAHE Bulletin*, March (39): 3–7. Washington, DC: American Association of Higher Education (AAHE). http://aahebulletin.com/public/archive/sevenprinciples1987.asp

Choi, H.J. and Johnson, S.D. (2006) The effect of problem-based video instruction on learner satisfaction, comprehension and retention in college students, *British Journal of Educational Technology*, 38: 885–95.

Coffey, A. and Atkinson, P. (1996) *Making Sence of Qualitative Data*. Thousand Oaks, CA: Sage.

Cohen, A.P. (1994) *Self Consciousness: An Alternative Anthropology of Identity*. Oxford: Routledge.

College of Marin (1990) Teacher directed classroom research. A Videotape, College of Marin, California.

Cousin, G. (2000) Strenthening action-research for educational development, *Educational Development*, 1(3).

Cowan, J. (2006) *On Becoming an Innovative University Teacher: Reflection in Action*, 2nd edn. Maidenhead: Open University Press/SRHE.

Creswell, J.W. (2002) *Research Design: Qualitative, Quantitative and Mixed Methods Approaches*, 2nd edn. London: Sage.

Creswell, J.W. (2007) *Qualitative Inquiry and Research Design: Choosing among five approaches*, 2nd edn. London: Sage.

Cronbach, L. and Suppes, P. (ed.) (1969) *Research for Tomorrow Schools: Disciplined Inquiry for Education*. New York: Macmillan.

Cross, K.P. (1987) The need for classroom research, in J.K. Kurfiss (ed.) *To Improve the Academy*. Stillwater, OK: POD Network in Higher Education and New Forums.

Cross, K.P. and Angelo, T. (1988) *Classroom Assessment Techniques: A Handbook for Faculty*. Ann Arbor, MI: National Center for Research to Improve Postsecondary Teaching and Learning, University of Michigan.

Cross, K.P. and Angelo, T. (1993a) *Classroom Assessment Techniques: A Handbook for College Teachers*, 2nd edn. San Francisco: Jossey-Bass.

Cross, K.P. and Angelo, T. (1993b) Teaching goals inventory, University of Iowa, Teaching Center. www.uiowa.edu/~centeach/tgi/index.html

Cross, K.P. and Steadman, M. (1996) *Classroom Research*. San Francisco, CA: Jossey-Bass.

Daiches, D. (ed.) (1964) *The Idea of a New University*. London: Deutsch.

D'Andrea, V. (2006) Exploring methodological issues related to pedagogic inquiry in Higher Education, in C. Kreber (ed.) *Exploring Research-based Teaching*. New Directions in Teaching and Learning no. 107. San Francisco: Jossey-Bass.

D'Andrea, V. and Gosling, D. (2005) *Improving Teaching and Learning in Higher Education: A Whole Institution Approach*. Maidenhead: Open University Press/ SRHE.

Davis, B. (1999) Fast feedback, *Tools for Teaching*. Berkeley, CA: University of California, Berkeley.

Deleuze, G. and Guattari, F. (1987) *A Thousand Plateaus*. Minneapolis: Minnesota University Press.

Denscombe, M. (2001) *The Good Research Guide: For Small-Scale Social Research Projects*, 2nd edn. Buckingham: Open University.

Denzin, N.K. and Lincoln, Y.S. (eds) (2007) *Strategies of Qualitative Inquiry*, 3rd edn. Thousand Oaks, CA: Sage.

Donald, J.G. (2002) *Learning to Think: Disciplinary Perspectives*. San Francisco: Jossey-Bass.

East, R. (2005) A progress report on progress files: the experience of one higher education institution, *Active Learning in Higher Education*, 6(2): 160–71.

Edgerton, R. (2005) Foreword, in K.O. Meara and R.E. Rice (eds) *Faculty Priorities Reconsidered: Rewarding Multiple Forms of Scholarship*. San Francisco, CA: Jossey-Bass.

Edgeworth, R.L. (1809) *Essays on Professional Education*. London: J. Johnson.

Eggins, H. and MacDonald, R. (2003) *The Scholarship of Academic Development*. Buckingham: Open University Press/SRHE.

Elbow, P. (1973) *Writing Without Teachers*. Oxford: Oxford University Press.

Engeström, Y. (ed.) (2001) Activity theory and social capital. Research reports 5, Center for Activity Theory and Development Work Research, Helsinki.

Entwistle, N. (1988) Motivational factors in students' approaches to learning, in R. Schmeck (ed.) *Learning Strategies and Learning Styles*. New York: Plenum.

Entwistle, N. (2005) Learning outcomes and ways of thinking across contrasting disciplines and settings in higher education, *The Curriculum Journal*, 16: 67–82.

Eraut, M. (1994) *Developing Professional Knowledge and Competence*. London: Falmer.

Exley, K. and Dennick, R. (2004) *Giving a Lecture: From Presenting to Teaching*. New York: Routledge Falmer.

Fanghanel, J. (2007) Teaching excellent in context: drawing from a socio-cultural approach, in A. Skelton (ed.) *International Perspectives on Teaching Excellence in Higher Education*. London: Routledge, pp. 197–212.

Finlay, I. (2003) Expansive learning across university and workplace activity systems: Learning to teach in further education, *International Journal of Learning*, 10.

Finlay, I., Holmes, S. and Kydd, L. (1998) Boundary management in further education: the case of Scottish FE colleges since incorporation, in R. Glatter and R. Levacic (eds) *Managing Change in Further Education*. London: Further Education Development Agency-The Open University.

Foley, D. (1998) On writing reflexive realist narratives, in G. Sherlock and J. Smyth (eds) *Being Reflexive in Critical Education and Social Research*. London: Falmer Press.

Freire, P. (1972) *Pedagogy of the Oppressed*. Harmondsworth: Penguin Education.

Fry, H., Ketteridge, S. and Marshall, S. (eds) (2008) *A Handbook for Teaching and Learning in Higher Education: Enhancing Academic Practice*, 3rd edn. Abingdon: Taylor & Francis.

Geertz, C. (1973) *The Interpretation of Culture*. New York: Basic Books.

Gibbs, G. and Jenkins, A. (eds) (1992) *Teaching Large Classes in Higher Education: How to Maintain Quality with Reduced Resources*. Abingdon: Routledge Falmer.

Glaser, B.G. and Strauss, S. ([1967] 1999) *The Discovery of Grounded Theory: Strategies for Qualitative Research*. Piscataway, NJ: State University of New Jersey, Aldine. Transaction.

Glassick, C., Huber, M. and Maeroff, G. (1997) *Scholarship Assessed: Evaluation of the Professoriate*. San Francisco, CA: Jossey-Bass.

Gray, H. (1999) *Universities and the Creation of Wealth*. Buckingham:/Open University Press/SRHE.

Häkkinen, P. (2002) Challenges for design of computer-based learning environments, *British Journal of Educational Technology*, 33(4): 461–9.

Halse, C., Deane, E., Hobson, J. and Jones, G. (2007) The research-teaching nexus: what do national teaching awards tell us? *Studies in Higher Education*, 32: 727–46.

Hart, C. (1998) *Doing a Literature Review: Releasing the Social Science Research Imagination*. London: Sage.

Hart, C. (2001) *Doing a Literature Search: A Comprehensive Guide for the Social Sciences*. London: Sage.

Healey, M. (2000) Developing the scholarship of teaching in higher education: a discipline-based approach, *Higher Education Research and Development*, 19: 169–89.

Henkel, M. (2000) *Academic Identities and Policy Change in Higher Education*. London: Jessica Kingsley.

HEA (Higher Education Academy) (2007) *The Higher Education Academy Annual Report 2006–07*. York: The Higher Education Academy.

Holmes et al. (2006) Deconstructing the evidence-based discourse in health sciences: truth, power and fascism, *International Journal of Evidence-Based Health*, 4: 180–6.

Huber, M. (2006) Disciplines, pedagogy and inquiry-based learning about teaching, in C. Kreber (ed.) *Exploring Research-based Teaching*. San Francisco: Jossey-Bass.

Huber, M. and Hutchings, P. (2005) *The Advancement of Learning: Building the Teaching Commons*. Stanford: The Carnegie Foundation.

Hutchings, P. (2004) The scholarship of teaching and learning in the United States. Paper presented to the International Society for the Scholarship of Teaching and Learning Conference, Bloomington, Indiana, Oct.

Huxam, M. (2005) Learning in lectures: do 'interactive windows' help? *Active Learning in Higher Education*, 6(1): 17–31.

Jaques, D. and Salmon, G. (2007) *Learning in Groups. A Handbook for Improving Group Work*, 3rd edn. London: Kogan Page.

Jarvis, P., Holford, J. and Griffin, C. (1998) *The Theory and Practice of Learning*. London: Kogan Page.

Jaspers, K. (1965) *The Idea of the University*. London: Peter Owen.

Jessup, G. (1991) *Outcomes: NVQs and the Emerging Model of Education and Training*. London: Falmer.

Jones, P. (2004) Finding the hospitality industry? Or finding hospitality schools of thought? *Journal of Hospitality, Leisure, Sport and Tourism Education*, 3(1): 33–45.

Jowett, A.K. (2005) Did the market force subject review? A case study, *Active Learning in Higher Education*, 6(1): 73–86.

Juwah, C., Macfarlane-Dick, D., Matthew, B., Nicol, D., Ross, D. and Smith, B. (2004) *Enhancing Student Learning through Effective Formative Feedback*. London: The Higher Education Academy Generic Centre.

Kelly, D.K. (1991) *The Effects of Classroom Research by Part-time Faculty upon the Retention of Adult Learners*. Saratoga Springs, NY: National Center on Adult Learning, Empire State College, SUNY.

Kelly, D.K. (1993) Classroom research and interactive learning: assessing the impact on adult learners and faculty. Unpublished doctoral dissertation, Claremont Graduate University.

Kerrins, J. and Cushing, K. (2000) Taking a second look: expert and novice differences when observing the same classroom teaching segment a second time, *Journal of Personnel Evaluation in Education*, 14(1): 5–24.

Knight, P. (2007) *Being a Teacher in Higher Education*, 2nd edn. Maidenhead: Open University Press/SRHE.

Kreber, C. (2003) The scholarship of teaching: a comparison of conceptions held by experts and regular academic staff, *Higher Education*, 46: 93–121.

Kreber, C. (2006) Promoting inquiry-based learning about teaching through educational development units, in C. Kreber (ed.) *Exploring Research-based Teaching*. New Directions in Teaching and Learning, no. 107. San Francisco: Jossey-Bass.

Kreber, C. and Hanuka, H. (2006) The scholarship of teaching and learning and the online classroom, *Canadian Journal of University Continuing Education*, 32(2): 109–31.

Land, R. (2004) *Educational Development*. Maidenhead: Open University Press/SRHE.

Lashley, C. (2004) Escaping the tyranny of relevance: some reflections on hospitality management education. Paper presented at the Council for Australian Tourism and Hospitality Education Conference, Brisbane.

Lashley, C., Lynch, P. and Morrison, A. (2007) *Hospitality: A Social Lens*. Elsevier: London.

Laurillard, D. (2002) *Rethinking University Teaching: A Conversational Framework for the Effective Use of Learning Technologies*, 2nd edn. Abingdon: Routledge-Falmer.

Lave, J. and Wenger, E. (1991) *Situated Learning: Legitimate Peripheral Participation*. Cambridge: Cambridge University Press.

Lea, M.R. and Stierer, B. (eds) (2000) *Student Writing in Higher Education: New Contexts*. Buckingham: Open University Press/SRHE.

Lettuca, L.R. (2002) Learning interdisciplinarity: sociocultural perspectives on academic work, *Journal of Higher Education* 73: 711–39.

Lettuca, L.R. (2005) Faculty work as learning: Insights from theories of cognition, in E.G. Creamer and L.R. Lettuca (eds) *Advancing Faculty Learning through Interdisciplinary Collaboration*. New Directions in Teaching and Learning no.102. San Francisco: Jossey-Bass.

Light, R. (1990) *The Harvard Assessment Seminars, First Report*. Cambridge, MA: Harvard University Graduate School of Education and Kennedy School of Government.

Lindblom-Ylänne, S., Trigwell, K., Nevgi, A. and Ashwin, P. (2006) How approaches to teaching are affected by discipline and teaching context, *Studies in Higher Education*, 31: 285–98.

Locke, J. (1693) *Some Thoughts Concerning Education*. www.fordham.edu/halsall/mod/1692locke-education.html (accessed 19 May 2008).

Lueddeke, G.R. (2003) Professionalising teaching practice in higher education: a study of disciplinary variation and 'teaching-scholarship', *Studies in Higher Education*, 28: 213–28.

Marton, F. (1981) Phenomenography: describing conceptions of the world around us, *Instructional Science*, 10: 177–200.

Marton, F. and Säljö, R. (1976) On qualitative differences in learning – 1: Outcome and process, *British Journal of Educational Psychology*, 46: 4–11.

Marton, F. and Säljö, R. (1997) Approaches to learning, in F. Marton, D. Hounsell and N.J. Entwistle (eds) *The Experience of Learning: Implications for Teaching and Studying in Higher Education*, 2nd edn. Edinburgh: Scottish Academic Press.

Maskell, D. and Robinson, D. (2001) *The New Idea of a University*. London: Haven Books.

McCarthy, L. (1994) A stranger in strange lands: a college student writing across the curriculum, in C. Bazerman and D. Russell (eds) *Landmark Essays on Writing Across the Curriculum*. Davis, CA: Hermagoras Press.

McCune, V. and Hounsell, D. (2005) The development of students ways of thinking and practicing in three final-year biology courses, *Higher Education*, 49: 255–89.

McKeachie, W. and Svinicki, M. (2006) *Teaching Tips: Strategies, Research and Theory for College and University Teachers*, 12th edn. Boston: Houghton Mifflin.

McKinney, K. (2004) The scholarship of teaching and learning: past lessons, current challenges and future visions, *To Improve the Academy*, 22: 3–19.

Meyer, E. and Land, R. (2003) Threshold concepts and troublesome knowledge (1): linkages to ways of thinking and practising within the disciplines, in C. Rust (ed.) *Improving Student Learning – Ten Years On*. Oxford: OCSLD.

Moon, J.A. (1999a) *Reflection in Learning and Professional Development: Theory and Practice*. London: Kogan Page.

Moon, J.A. (1999b) *Learning Journals: A Handbook for Academics, Students and Professional Development*. London: Kogan Page.

Morling, B., McAuliffe, M., Cohen, L. and DiLorenzo, T.M. (2008) Efficacy of personal response systems ('Clickers') in large introductory psychology classes, *Teaching of Psychology*, 35: 45–50.

Morrison, A. and O'Gorman, K. (2007) Hospitality studies and hospitality management: a symbiotic relationship, *International Journal of Hospitality Management*. doi:10.1016/j.ijhm.2007.07.028: 1–8.

Morrison, A. and O'Mahony, B. (2003) The liberation of hospitality management education, *International Journal of Contemporary Hospitality Management*, 15(1): 38–44.

Morse, J.M. (ed.) (1994) *Critical Issues in Qualitative Research Methods*. Thousand Oaks, CA: Sage.

Morss, K. and Murray, R. (2001) Researching academic writing within a structured programme: insights and outcomes, *Studies in Higher Education*, 26(1): 35–52.

Morss, K. and Murray, R. (2005) *Teaching at University: A Guide for Postgraduates and Researchers*. London: Sage.

Mosteller, F. (1989) The 'muddiest point in the lecture' as a feedback device, *On Teaching and Learning 3*. Cambridge, MA: Harvard University, Derek Bok Center for Teaching and Learning. http://bokcenter.fas.harvard.edu/docs/mosteller.html

Murray, R. (2003) Students' questions and their implications for the viva, *Quality Assurance in Education*, 11(2): 109–13.

Murray, R. (2006) *How to Write a Thesis*, 2nd edn. Maidenhead: Open University Press.

Murray, R. and Newton, M. (2008) Facilitating writing for publication, *Physiotherapy*, 94: 29, 34.

Murray, R., Thow, M., Moore, S. and Murphy, M. (2008) The writing consultation: developing academic writing practices, *Journal of Further and Higher Education*, 32(2): 119–28.

Nathan, R. (2005) *My Freshman Year: What a Professor Learned by Becoming a Student*. Ithaca, NY: Cornell University Press.

Newman, J. (1976 [based on 9th edn. 1889]) *The Idea of a University*. Oxford: Clarendon Press.

OECD (1972) *Interdisciplinarity: Problems of Teaching and Research in Universities*. Paris: OECD.

O Meara, K. and Rice, R.E. (2005) *Faculty Priorities Reconsidered: Rewarding Multiple Forms of Scholarship*. San Francisco, CA: Jossey-Bass.

Patton, M.Q. (1986) *Utilization-Focused Evaluation*, 2nd edn. Thousand Oaks, CA: Sage.

Patton, M.Q. (2001) *Qualitative Research and Evaluation Methods*, 3rd edn. Thousand Oaks, CA: Sage.

Peake, G. (2006) *Observation of the Practice of Teaching: Research Findings from the FDTL5 Project at University of Hull Consortium for PCET*. http://escalate.ac.uk/3060 (accessed 12 May 2008).

Pelikan, J. (1992) *The Idea of the University: A Re-examination*. New Haven, CT: Yale University Press.

Pellino, G., Blackburn, R. and Boberg, A. (1984) The dimensions of academic scholarship: faculty and administrator views, *Research in Higher Education*, 20(1): 103–15.

Polanyi, M. (1958) *Personal Knowledge: Towards a Post-Critical Philosophy*. London: Routledge and Kegan Paul.

Polanyi, M. (1959) *The Study of Man*. London: Routledge and Kegan Paul.

Prosser, M. and Trigwell, K. (1999) *Understanding Learning and Teaching: The Experience in Higher Education*. Buckingham: Open University Press/SRHE.

Prosser, M., Rickinson, M., Bence, V., Hanbury, A. and Kulej, M. (2006) *Formative Evaluation of Accredited Programmes*. York: Higher Education Academy.

Race, P. (2001) *The Lecturer's Toolkit: A Practical Guide to Learning, Teaching and Assessment*. London: Kogan Page.

Ramsden, P. (2003) *Learning to Teach in Higher Education*, 2nd edn. London: Routledge.

Ritchie, J. and Lewis, J. (eds) (2003) *Qualitative Research Practice: A Guide for Social Science Students and Researchers*. London: Sage.

Rogers, A. (2002) *Teaching Adults*, 3rd edn. Buckingham: Open University Press.

Roueche, S. (ed.) (1993) What I learned about quality in the classroom from a Harvard Business School professor and a group of freshman students, *Innovation*

Abstracts XV (22). Austin, TX: National Institute for Staff and Organizational Development (NISOD), College of Education, University of Texas at Austin.

Rowland, S. (2006) *The Enquiring University: Compliance and Contestation in Higher Education.* Maidenhead: Open University Press/SRHE.

Ryan, A. (1999) *Liberal Anxieties and Liberal Education: What Education is Really For and Why It Matters.* London: Profile Books.

Sadler, D. (1989) Formative assessment and the design of instructional systems, *Instructional Science,* 18: 119–44.

Salmon, G. (2003) *E-Moderating: The Key to Teaching and Learning Online,* 2nd edn. Routledge: London.

Schön, D. (1995) *The Reflective Practitioner.* San Francisco, CA: Jossey-Bass.

Sfard, A. (1998) On two metaphors for learning and on the dangers of choosing just one, *Educational Researcher,* 27(2): 4–13.

Shank, G.D. (2002) *Qualitative Research: A Personal Skills Approach.* Columbus, OH: Merrill Prentice Hall.

Shulman, L. (1987) Knowledge and teaching: Foundations of the new reform. *Harvard Educational Review,* 36(1): 1–22.

Shulman, L. (1993) Teaching as community property: putting an end to pedagogical solitude, *Change,* Nov./Dec. 25(6): 6–7.

Shulman, L. (1998) Course anatomy: the dissection and analysis of knowledge through teaching, in P. Hutchings (ed.) *The Course Portfolio: How Faculty Can Examine Their Teaching to Advance Practice and Improve Student Learning.* Washington, DC: American Association for Higher Education.

Shulman, L. (1999) Taking learning seriously, *Change,* 31(4): 10–17.

Shulman, L. and Hutchings, P. (1999) The scholarship of teaching: new elaborations, new developments, *Change,* 31(5): 10–15.

Shulman, L.S. (2004) Disciplines of inquiry in education, *The Wisdom of Practice.* San Francisco: Jossey-Bass.

Shulman, L.S. (2005) Signature pedagogies in the professions, *Daudalus,* 52–9.

Silverman, D. (ed.) (2004) *Qualitative Research: Theory, Method and Practice,* 2nd edn. London: Sage.

Silverman, D. (2006) *Interpreting Qualitative Data,* 3rd edn. London: Sage.

Simons, H. (1980) *Towards a Science of the Singular.* Norwich: University of East Anglia.

Sinclair, C. (2004) Students and discourse: an insider perspective. Unpublished PhD thesis, Open University.

Sinclair, C. (2008) Confessions of a Mechanical Engineering student, in P. Frame and J. Burnett (eds) *Using Auto/Biography in Teaching and Learning.* London: Staff and Educational Development Association.

Skelton, A. (ed.) (2007) *International Perspectives on Teaching Excellence in Higher Education: Improving Knowledge and Practice.* London: Routledge.

Skerratt, S. (2008), The persistence of place: the importance of shared participation environments when deploying ICTs in rural areas, in G. Rusten and S. Skerratt,D (eds), *Information & Communication Technologies in rural society: Being Rural in a Digital Age.* Oxford: Routledge.

Spears, M. and Gregoire, M. (2007) *Foodservice Organisations: A Managerial and Systems Approach.* New Jersey: Pearson-Prentice Hall.

Spencer, L., Ritchie, J., Lewis, J. and Dillon, L. (2003) *Quality in Qualitative Evaluation: A Framework for Assessing Research Evidence.* London: Cabinet Office. www.gsr.gov.uk/downloads/evaluating_policy/a_quality_framework.pdf

Spencer, M. and Kent, P. (2007) Perpetuating difference? Law school sabbaticals in the era of performativity, *Legal Studies*, 27(4): 649–77.

Stake, R.E. (1995) *The Art of Case Study Research.* Thousand Oaks. CA: Sage.

Strachan, R., Murray, R. and Grierson, H. (2004) A web-based tool for dissertation writing, *British Journal of Educational Technology*, 35(3): 369–75.

Svensson, L. (1989) The conceptualization of cases of physical motion, *European Journal of Psychology of Education*, 4(4): 529–45.

Tight, M. (2003) *Researching Higher Education.* Maidenhead: Open University Press/ SRHE.

Toohey, S. (1999) *Designing Courses for Higher Education.* Buckingham: Open University Press/SRHE.

Trahar, S. (2007) *Teaching and Learning: The International Higher Education Landscape – Some Theories and Working Practice. ESCalate.* http://escalate.ac.uk/2018 (accessed 12 May 2008).

Tribe, J. (2002) The philosophic practitioner, *Annals of Tourism Research*, 29(2): 338–57.

Vygotsky, L.S. ([1934] 1987) Thinking and speech, in R.W. Rieber and A.S. Carton (eds) *The Collected Works of L.S. Vygotsky.* Vol. 1. New York and London: Plenum.

Wagner, J. (2007) Constructing credible images: documentary studies, social research and visual studies, *American Behavioral Scientists*, Special Issue, 47(12).

Walker, M. (2006) *Higher Education Pedagogies.* Maidenhead: Open University Press/ SRHE.

Wenger, E. (1998) *Communities of Practice: Learning, Meaning and Identity.* Cambridge: Cambridge University Press.

Whitehead, A.N. (1950) *The Aims of Education and Other Essays*, new edn. London: Williams and Norgate.

Index

LIBRARY, UNIVERSITY OF CHESTER

TEACHING FOR QUALITY LEARNING AT UNIVERSITY

Third Edition

John Biggs and Catherine Tang

'This book is a sophisticated and insightful conceptualization of outcomes-based learning developed from the concept of constructive alignment. The first author has already made a significant contribution to the scholarship and practice of teaching and learning in universities ...Together with the second author, there is now added richness through the practical implementation and practices. The ideas in this book are all tried and shown to contribute to more successful learning experience and outcome for students.'

Denise Chalmers, Carrick Institute of Education, Australia

Teaching for Quality Learning at University focuses on implementing a constructively aligned outcomes-based model at both classroom and institutional level. The theory, which is now used worldwide as a framework for good teaching and assessment, is shown to:

- Assist university teachers who wish to improve the quality of their own teaching, their students' learning and their assessment of learning outcomes
- Aid staff developers in providing support for teachers
- Provide a framework for administrators interested in quality assurance and enhancement of teaching across the whole university

The book's 'how to' approach addresses several important issues: designing high level outcomes, the learning activities most likely to achieve them in small and large classes, and appropriate assessment and grading procedures. It is an accessible, jargon-free guide to all university teachers interested in enhancing their teaching and their students' learning, and for administrators and teaching developers who are involved in teaching-related decisions on an institution-wide basis. The authors have also included useful web links to further material.

Contents: List of boxes – List of figures – List of tables – List of tasks – Foreword to original edition – Preface to third edition – Acknowledgements – When you have read this book – The changing scene in university teaching – Teaching according to how students learn – Setting the stage for effective teaching – Using constructive alignment in outcomes-based teaching and learning – Designing intended learning outcomes – Contexts for effective teaching and learning – Teaching/learning activities for declarative knowledge – Teaching/learning activities for functioning knowledge – Aligning Assessment with intended learning outcomes: Principles – Assessing and grading declarative knowledge – Assessing and grading functioning knowledge – Implementing constructive alignment – Constructive alignment as implemented: Some examples – References – Index.

2007 360pp

978-0-335-22126-4 (Paperback)

FACILITATING REFLECTIVE LEARNING IN HIGHER EDUCATION

Second Edition

Anne Brockbank and Ian McGill

Praise for the previous edition:

"This is a passionate and practical book"

Teaching in Higher Education

"This book offers valuable insights into a process for becoming a reflective learner and for developing students into reflective learners as well."

Studies in Higher Education

This significantly revised edition includes the most current thinking on reflective learning as well as stories from academics and students that bring to life the practical impact of reflection in action. Based on sound theoretical concepts, the authors offer a range of solutions for different teaching situations, taking into account factors such as group size, physical space, and technology. They also offer facilitation rather than traditional teaching methods as a productive and useful skill that helps teachers and encourages students to interact and develop reflexive skills that can be used beyond their student years.

Based on rigorous theories, *Facilitating Reflective Learning in Higher Education* offers new insights for university and college teachers seeking to enhance or diversify their practices and allows them to effectively facilitate their students' reflective learning.

Contents: *Acknowledgements – Introduction to the second edition – Part I Learning and reflection – Our themes – Learning philosophies and principles – What is learning? A review of learning theories – Requirements for reflection – Reflection and reflective practice – Part II Facilitating learning and reflective practice – Academic practice and learning – Methods of reflection for tutors – Methods and assessment of reflective learning – Becoming a facilitator: Enabling reflective learning – Facilitation in practice: Basic skills – Facilitation in practice: Further skills – Part III Exemplars – Action learning (learning sets) – Academic supervision – Mentoring – Conclusion – Appendices – Bibliography – Index.*

2007 384pp

978-0-335-22091-5 (Paperback) 978-0-335-22092-2 (Hardback)